AN AGENDA
FOR THE NATION

AN AGENDA FOR THE NATION

An Untold Story of the UPA Government

Pushpa M Bhargava & Chandana Chakrabarti

Foreword by **Prashant Bhushan**

MAPIN PUBLISHING

First published in India in 2014 by
Mapin Publishing Pvt. Ltd

Simultaneously published in the
United States of America in 2014 by
Grantha Corporation
E: mapin@mapinpub.com

Distributed in North America by
Antique Collectors' Club
T: 1 800 252 5231 • F: 413 529 0862
E: sales@antiquecc.com • www.accdistribution.com/us

Distributed in United Kingdom and Europe by
Gazelle Book Services Ltd.
T: 44 1524-68765 • F: 44 1524-63232
E: sales@gazellebooks.co.uk • www.gazellebookservices.co.uk

Distributed in Southeast Asia by
Paragon Asia Co. Ltd
T: 66 2877 7755 • F: 66 2468 9636
E: info@paragonasia.com

Distributed in the rest of the world by
Mapin Publishing Pvt. Ltd
706 Kaivanna, Panchvati, Ellisbridge,
Ahmedabad 380006 INDIA
T: 91 79 4022 8228 • F: 91 79 4022 8201
E: mapin@mapinpub.com • www.mapinpub.com

ISBN: 978-81-89995-90-4 (Mapin)
ISBN: 978-1-935677-45-1 (Grantha)
LCCN: 2014931265

Copyediting: Mallika Sarabhai and Neha Manke/Mapin Editorial
Design: Gopal Limbad/Mapin Design Studio
Production: Mapin Design Studio

Printed by Parksons Graphics, Mumbai

FOREWORD

India is a country blessed with more than adequate natural and human resources. We have adequate minerals of all kinds; adequate forest wealth; amazing biodiversity; geographical diversity; long coastline; the biggest range of mountains; unmatched human diversity, a wealth of highly evolved languages; unique cuisine; an unparalleled range of foods, fruits and vegetables; and the largest pool of young people who are capable of working hard in great adversity. And yet, despite all this wealth, we remain among the poorest countries in the world with the highest levels of malnutrition, especially among children; lack of clean drinking water and sanitation; lack of basic healthcare facilities; lack of educational facilities; and lack of decent housing. Though we have shown impressive GDP growth recently, we have in the same period slid down the Human Development Index, moving below even Bangladesh, Nepal and Sri Lanka.

The reason for this paradox lies in our poor governance and appalling levels of corruption which have made India one of the most corrupt countries in the world in the Transparency International Corruption Perception Index. This has led to policies drawn not in public interest but for benefitting vested commercial interests, which has led to a situation where most of our assets have been unutilized, misutilised and even plundered for corrupt considerations, leading to unprecedented levels of inequalities which have reduced democracy virtually to a farce.

Dr P M Bhargava and Mrs Chandana Chakrabarti are among the most sensitized, knowledgeable and best-qualified persons to think about the problems of the country and their solutions in terms of public policy prescriptions and fixes required in the governance systems and structures of the country. Dr Bhargava has not only been one of the most eminent scientists and institution builders in the country, he has also had the opportunity to be a member of many, perhaps most of the policy recommending institutions in the country, particularly those relating to science and technology. It is from that vantage point and concern that he initiated a process of getting some of the best and most sensitive minds together to draw up "An Agenda for the Nation", for the purpose of preparing policy prescriptions in all areas affecting the country and its people, including agriculture, education, health, energy, environment and, particularly, governance itself. They went about the job very scientifically and methodically by first identifying our natural, human, social and man-made assets, then prioritizing our problems and, following that, seeking appropriate policies which could best utilize our assets to solve our problems. The agenda that they drew up included many salutary measures:

Governance: Decentralisation of power; bringing in more transparency in the functioning of public authorities, particularly by using Information Technology; bringing more accountability by bringing an independent and empowered Lokpal; police and civil service reforms to insulate to some extent these services from the strangulating control of their political bosses, without compromising their accountability.

Electoral reforms: Introducing proportional representation; the right to reject; disallowing candidates with criminal antecedents; public funding of candidates based on some well-defined criteria; transparency of political parties, etc.

Agriculture: Leveraging and using our wealth of fruits and vegetables; using traditional knowledge and developing medicinal plants; promoting organic farming for healthier food and sustainable agriculture; adopting rainwater harvesting for improving irrigation; promoting indigenous seeds and preventing corporate control over seeds; avoiding untested genetically modified seeds which threaten our biodiversity; value addition of agricultural produce by promoting food processing and food preservation and marketing of the processed food; promoting the use of biomass as a source of energy, etc.

Education: Ensuring adequate good quality government schools which can accommodate all children by vastly increasing the funding for education; promoting a common school system so that the children of the elite also study in these schools which will ensure that the quality of the government schools is maintained; bringing the curriculum of schools in line with the national curriculum framework to ensure that rote learning is changed to developing the capacity for critical thinking and reasoning; vastly increasing the number of government-funded universities and creating an independent apex body for ensuring proper standards in these universities, etc.

Health: Greater emphasis on prevention, by using traditional systems of medicine and yoga; greatly increasing public funding of healthcare, particularly primary health centres which can be manned by paramedics; promoting the use of general physicians who can then refer patients to specialists only if required; decommercialising healthcare, etc.

The book deals with many more critical issues of policy. It is an extremely useful document for anyone who seeks an understanding of the major problems facing the nation and their solutions. The book also documents the unfortunate saga of how the UPA government did not implement virtually any of the policy prescriptions suggested by Dr Bhargava and the team of eminent people who had worked on this agenda, which substantially overlapped with the Congress Party's manifesto for the 2004 elections and with the Common Minimum Programme of UPA-1 Government. All of this seems to have been sacrificed at the altar of the mania of "GDP growth" at any cost and the commercial interest of crony capitalists who had this government under their control. It is not only a great opportunity lost, but also that the rampant loot that has gone on has brought us to an impasse where this country stands at the brink of economic, social and environmental collapse, virtually at the brink of anarchy. Let us hope that a resurgent civil society in the country will be able to challenge the corrupt political forces in control of the ruling establishment today and we will see a new order: an order which will see the wisdom of many policies outlined in this book and will follow them so that the suffering people of this country can be delivered from their misery and we can create a just and happy society.

Prashant Bhushan
4 November 2013

AUTHORS' NOTE

→ Part I of this book documents the events since Independence that led to the preparation of the Agenda for the Nation described briefly in the next paragraph, and its presentation to the top leadership of the Congress Party at 10 Janpath, the residence of its President, Mrs Sonia Gandhi, in December 2003.

→ Part II of the book documents in a summary form (perhaps for the first time), as of 2003, our national assets, our problems/liabilities and their interrelationships, to identify those at the top of the problem hierarchy. What kind of citizens would we like to have? What quality of life and lifestyles do we wish to achieve in our various sectors (such as rural, urban or tribal)? What are the steps the UPA Government ought to have taken since it came to power in early 2004, to use our assets to overcome our problems so that we could reach the destination we had defined, without compromising on the values that we would like our citizens to have? This part of the book has been called "An Agenda for the Nation: Expectations from the United Progressive Alliance (UPA) Government in 2004".

→ Part III of the book states in a summary form what has been actually achieved as of 2012 with respect to the expectations raised in Part II. It is titled "Successes and failures of the UPA Government between 2004 and 2012". The conclusion (Part IV: Epilogue) is: Accomplishments Are Few, Failures Many.

→ Part V of the book states some important action points for the Government as of April 2013, which were brought to the notice of the Prime Minister between July and November 2012, and on which again very little, if any, action has been taken.

→ The book should be of help to those who govern in the future, as well as to those who are governed.

→ The book does not claim to be comprehensive or exhaustive. The authors welcome suggestions for additions, deletions or modifications. The authors also recognize that there may be other—even better—modes of presentation of the material contained in the book.

Pushpa M Bhargava

bhargava.pm@gmail.com

Chandana Chakrabarti

chandana.chakrabarti@gmail.com

C O N T E N T S

OF THE UPA GOVERNMENT BETWEEN 2004 AND 2012

FURTHER STEPS NEEDED AS OF MAY 2013, IN ADDITION TO THOSE STATED IN PART II, TO SOLVE SOME OF OUR MAJOR PROBLEMS

ABBREVIATIONS

- Some well-known abbreviations may not appear in this list.
- Some technical abbreviations have not been included.
- Abbreviations that have become an acronym have also not been included.

AICRP	All India Coordinated Research Project
AICTE	All India Council for Technical Education
AIDS	Auto Immune Deficiency Syndrome
AP	Andhra Pradesh
ASHA	Accredited Social Health Activist
AYUSH	Department of Ayurveda, Yoga & Naturopathy, Unani, Siddha and Homeopathy
BJP	Bharatiya Janata Party
BRAI	Biotechnology Regulatory Authority of India
CCMB	Centre for Cellular and Molecular Biology
CCRHS	Centre for Conflict Resolution & Human Security
CIAE	Central Institute of Agricultural Engineering, Bhopal
CICR	Central Institute of Cotton Research
CID	Criminal Investigation Department
CME	Continuing Medical Education
CMP	Common Minimum Programme
CS	Crop Science
CSD	Council for Social Development
CSIR	Council of Scientific and Industrial Research
DARE	Department of Agricultural Research and Education
DBT	Department of Biotechnology
Dept	Department
DG	Director General
DNA	Deoxyribonucleic Acid

DST	Department of Science and Technology
EG	East Godavari (District)
Ento.	Entomology
ESOP	Employee Stock Ownership Plan
ETS	Educational Testing Service
FCI	Food Corporation of India
FDI	Foreign Direct Investment
FEI	Foreign Educational Institution
FEP	Foreign Education Provider
FM	Frequency Modulation
FMV	Foot and Mouth Virus
FRA	Forest Dwellers Rights Act
FRLHT	Foundation for Revitalisation of Local Health Traditions
GAP	Good Agricultural Practice
GCP	Good Clinical Practice
GDP	Gross Domestic Product
GEAC	Genetic Engineering Appraisal (earlier Approval) Committee
GHP	Good Harvesting Practice
GLP	Good Laboratory Practice
GM	Genetically Modified
GMO	Genetically Modified Organism
GMP	Good Manufacturing Practice
GOI	Government of India
GP	General Physician
HC	High Court
HERA	Higher Education Regulatory Authority
HORDI	Horticulture Crop Research and Development Institute, Sri Lanka
Hort.	Horticulture
IARI	Indian Agricultural Research Institute
IAS	Indian Administrative Service

ICAR	Indian Council of Agricultural Research
ICT	Information and Communication Technology
IEI	Indian Educational Institution
IGNOU	Indira Gandhi National Open University
IISc	Indian Institute of Science
IIT	Indian Institute of Technology
IPM	Integrated Pest Management
IPR	Intellectual Property Rights
IPS	Indian Police Service
ITI	Industrial Training Institute
KVKs	Kisan Vikas Kendras
L&T	Larsen & Toubro
LCD	Liquid Crystal Display
MCI	Medical Council of India
MD	Managing Director
MHRD	Ministry of Human Resource Development
MLA	Member of Legislative Assembly
MNCs	Multinational Companies
MNES	Ministry of Non-conventional Energy Sources
MoU	Memorandum of Understanding
MP	Member of Parliament
MSSRF	M S Swaminathan Research Foundation
NAAS	National Academy of Agricultural Sciences
NABH	National Accreditation Board for Hospitals & Healthcare Providers
NABL	National Accreditation Board for Testing and Calibration Laboratories
NAC	National Advisory Council
NASSCOM	National Association of Software and Services Companies
NCF	National Commission on Farmers
NCIPM	National Research Centre for Integrated Pest Management
NGO	Non Governmental Organisation

NHRC	National Human Rights Commission
NIF	National Innovation Foundation
NKC	National Knowledge Commission
NOC	No Objection Certificate
NPA	National Police Academy
NPM	Non-Pesticide Management
NREGS	National Rural Employment Guarantee Scheme
NRSA	National Remote Sensing Agency
OBCs	Other Backward Communities
OTC	Over-the-counter
PC	Producer Company
PDS	Public Distribution System
PESA	Panchayat Extension to Scheduled Areas Act
PG	Post-graduate
Pl. Path.	Plant Pathology
PP	Plant Protection
PPA	Plant Protection Adviser
PSU	Public Service Undertaking
R&D	Research and Development
REN	Rural Enterprise Network, Sri Lanka
S&T	Science and Technology
SEZs	Special Economic Zones
SHG	Self Help Group
SNPs	Single-nucleotide polymorphism
SOP	Standard Operating Procedure
TB	Tuberculosis
TDP	Telugu Desam Party
TERI	The Energy Research Institute
The MARCH	The Medically Aware and Responsible Citizens of Hyderabad
TK	Traditional knowledge
TRIPS	Trade-Related Aspects of Intellectual Property Rights

UGC	University Grants Commission
UHC	Universal Health Coverage
UPA	United Progressive Alliance
UPOV	International Union for the Protection of New Varieties of Plants
V-C	Vice-Chancellor
VPKAS	Vivekanand Parvatiya Krishi Anusandhan Shala
WTO	World Trade Organisation

I

THE HISTORY

Narrated by **Pushpa M Bhargava**

1945-1950

Those were heady years for those of us who were adults and were preparing to embark on our professional careers in the new India. We shared Jawaharlal Nehru's dream of a great independent India—an India that would make Thomas More's Utopia come alive.

Come 1970s

Our country had produced great leaders in every area of human endeavour during the preceding quarter century. (By contrast, we have a crisis of leadership today in every sphere—be it science or politics.) Our commitment to self-reliance and to political independence enshrined in our policy of non-alignment had, then, set India apart from every other country. And we were till that time, virtually corruption-free if viewed against the deeply embedded streak of corruption everywhere in the country today. This was also about the time that education began to be commercialized.

And we began to be disillusioned. Where was the India of our dreams? We realized that no one, including Jawaharlal Nehru (whom I had the privilege of meeting on several occasions), had ever defined operationally what kind of lifestyles we envisaged for our citizens. Clearly, they wouldn't be the same in villages, in small urban areas, and in metropolises, or for our tribals. And we had never stated, succinctly and comprehensively, what kind of citizens we would like to have. True, Mahatma Gandhi's teachings and statements (like those of several others) gave us an inkling of that, but the picture that emerged from such teachings and statements did not allow one to define courses of action to achieve the stated objectives.

For the next three decades, we had a prolonged and intense discussion among many of the leading intellectuals and thinkers in the country about preparing a document to be called 'An Agenda for the Nation', which would have the following components that we slowly realized had never before been comprehensively stated, even individually, leave aside collectively.

- Our assets.
- Our problems and their inter-relationships (how they impacted each other) that would identify the problems at the top of the problem hierarchy so that if they were not solved, other problems would never be solved adequately.
- What kind of citizens we wish to have.
- What kind of lifestyles we envisage for our citizens in urban, rural and tribal areas.
- What steps we may take so that we may use our assets optimally to overcome our problems, to reach the destination (the lifestyles) we have defined, without compromising on the values we believe our citizens should have.
- The criteria that we may use to assess the success of the actions taken to reach the destination we have defined.

Some of the people involved in the discussion who, unfortunately, are no longer with us were: Mohit Sen, one of the most prominent ideological leaders of the communist movement in the country; Nikhil Chakravarthy, Editor of *Mainstream*; Sukhamoy Chakravarty, distinguished economist; N P Sen, Chairman of Indian Airlines and of Food Corporation of India, who was also the Principal of the Administrative Staff College of India at Hyderabad; Satish Dhawan, Secretary, Department of Space, and Chairman, Indian Space Research Organisation; I G Patel, Director of London School of Economics and Governor of Reserve Bank of India; K G Kannabiran, a well-known human rights activist; and Rasheeduddin Khan, Member of Parliament.

To achieve the above objective, we felt that we should get together some 50 persons (like those mentioned above) who satisfied these criteria:

- They had achieved a high level of success in their own profession or avocation.
- They had high public credibility.
- Their integrity and honesty were undisputed.
- They had a strong social commitment.
- They were articulate.
- They were amenable to dialogue and discussion.

We were initially told by friends and well-wishers that it would be difficult to find fifty such persons in the country but we actually made a list of a hundred!

But then the question of funds arose. What we had planned was to have these fifty people live together for a week, working long hours every day, at an isolated place so that no one could take time out to meet another commitment. For this, at that time (in the early 1980s), we needed approximately Rs.10 lakh to take care of the travel, stay and other expenses of the above group. The expected outcome was to be a 50-page document which would incorporate what has been mentioned above.

To raise the above money, I met Inder Gujral who was then the Prime Minister (which meeting was arranged by NN Vohra, the well-known bureaucrat who was then the Director of India International Centre and later became our interlocutor in Kashmir, and who had supported the idea of preparing An Agenda for the Nation); Rajiv Gandhi; and, after Rajiv Gandhi's assassination, Sonia Gandhi. Everyone commended the idea but something or the other prevented it from taking shape. Gujral lost the elections. Rajiv Gandhi was assassinated. Sonia Gandhi did ask Abid Husain (our former Ambassador to the United States and, then, the Vice-President of Rajiv Gandhi Foundation) to pursue the matter, and one late evening I did get a call from him to send him names of some twenty five people for a meeting to be organized in Delhi itself, which list we sent him by fax at about midnight the same day. However, almost immediately afterwards Abid left the Rajiv Gandhi Foundation under the auspices of which, ostensibly, the meeting was supposed to be held, and the matter was not followed up.

After these disappointments, Mohit Sen suggested the possibility of the Congress Party supporting the above exercise, with the understanding that the document that emerges will be made available to all the political parties. Soon, the two of us met Manmohan Singh who was then the Leader of Opposition in the Rajya Sabha, suggesting that he put up the proposal to the Congress Working Committee. Sitaram Kesari was then the President of the Indian National Congress.

We were not amused when, later, one day, Manmohan Singh told us that when he put up the proposal to the Congress Working Committee, Sitaram Kesari said to him in Hindi, "Doctor Saheb, please understand that politics is not a matter of the brain; it is a matter of the heart. And you should keep away from those brainy fellows!". (In Hindi: "*Doctor Saheb, ye jo politics hai, ye dimag ka mamla nahi hai; ye dil ka mamla hai. Aur aap in dimag walo se door rahiye!*".) Time lapsed and we lost Mohit on 4th May 2003. Ironically, a few weeks later, after I had become a life member of the Council for Social Development (CSD) in Delhi, which had been set up by C D Deshmukh and Durgabhai Deshmukh, and which was then presided over by the former Foreign Secretary, Muchkund Dubey, CSD agreed to sponsor the preparation of the proposed Agenda for the Nation. After meetings held under the auspices of CSD, and with special inputs from Jayaprakash Narayan (who had left the Indian Administrative Service and founded what is now the Loksatta Party in Andhra Pradesh), and EAS Sarma (a former Secretary to the Government of India and then the Principal of the Administrative Staff College of India), the document, prepared by Chandana Chakrabarti and me, was finalized and frozen in September 2003. It was titled "An Agenda for the Nation", and is referred to as "the Agenda" or 'the document' later on. Before I proceed further, Chandana and I must record our deep sense of gratitude to CSD (specially its President, Muchkund Dubey) and to Jayaprakash Narayan and EAS Sarma, without whose deep involvement and commitment the document would have never seen the light of the day.

As I have said earlier, it was an irony that Mohit Sen had passed away some four months earlier. He had been one of the most ardent advocates of such a document for nearly two decades, and his presence would have, no doubt, lessened the shortcomings of the document we are presenting in Part II of this book.

On 28th August 2003, I gave the document (the Agenda) to Manmohan Singh who was then the Leader of Opposition in the Rajya Sabha and was living at 19 Safdarjung Road (New Delhi). He apparently read it, perhaps saw some merit in it and, therefore, forwarded it to Sonia Gandhi who had by then taken over as the President of the Indian National Congress from Sitaram Kesari. On 22nd October 2003, when I was in Chennai, I got a call from her office enquiring if Manmohan Singh and I could see her about the document. Consequently, the two of us saw her at 10 Janpath on the 24th October. When we entered the room, she was standing with the document in her hand and said to me that she thought the document was fantastic. She then asked Manmohan Singh as to what could be done with the document. He replied saying that the manifesto for the elections in four states (Delhi, Rajasthan, Madhya Pradesh and Chhattisgarh) which were scheduled to be held within the next two months, had been finalized. Therefore, it may be a good idea to use the document for the General Elections in 2004. She then asked me if I would be willing to make a presentation of the document to her leadership after the elections in the four states were over. When I said yes, she suggested that I do so in December 2003 after the results of the elections in the above four states were out.

Incidentally, on 14th October 2003, I also had occasion to present a copy of the Agenda to Swami Chinmayananda, then Minister of State in the Home Ministry of the Bharatiya Janata Party (BJP)-led Government, when I met him at his residence at his invitation in another connection. After hearing me out about the contents of the document, he told me that I should really give it to Jaswant Singh. When I replied saying that I did not know Jaswant Singh, he did not reply. We never heard of it again from the BJP side, and I would not be surprised if he put the document in the waste paper basket after I had left.

What happened after the meeting at 10 Janpath on 24th October 2003 is history. The Congress Party lost the elections in the following few weeks rather badly in three states, and won only in Delhi. From all accounts one has, the Party was, subsequently, in shambles, without the slightest hope of winning in the 2004 elections, and I felt sure that Sonia Gandhi would have forgotten about our document.

But she didn't. On 23rd December, 2003, while I was having lunch with Ashish Modi of Shivani Scientific Instruments Private Ltd. at his residence, I got a call from her office asking if I could make the presentation I had promised earlier, of the Agenda, on 29th December that year at 10 Janpath. Immediately after the call, I got a call from Manmohan Singh enquiring if I had heard from Mrs Gandhi. I confirmed that I had, and that the date (and the time: 5.30 pm) was alright with me. I then let Sonia Gandhi's office know that I will be accompanied by my colleague, Chandana Chakrabarti, who had co-authored the Agenda, Prof. Muchkund Dubey, President of CSD that had been instrumental in preparing the Agenda, and Dr M D Asthana who was then the Director of CSD.

Later I called her office to say that I had three requirements:
   a. that there would be no time limit for presentation and, therefore, all those who may be participating in the event should not have anything scheduled after the event;

b. that since so much effort of so many people over such a long period had gone into preparing the document, it would be only fair to expect that those who come for its presentation will stay on till the end of the presentation;

c. that we would need an LCD projector and a projectionist.

The first two conditions were immediately agreed to but we were told that 10 Janpath had no LCD projector. It was not easy to organize one as it would have been quite a task to hire a projectionist without telling him where we were going to take him with his projector. There was the question of his security clearance (10 Janpath is like a fortress), and we also intuitively knew that it would not be appropriate to let anyone else know at that time about the presentation. As it turned out, 10 Janpath did finally organize the LCD projector for us.

Our presentation started as scheduled at 5.30 pm and took about two-and-a-half hours. Our audience consisted of Sonia Gandhi, Manmohan Singh, Natwar Singh, Jairam Ramesh, Ahmed Patel, Pranab Mukherjee, and Mani Shankar Aiyer, five of whom later became Members of the Council of Ministers of the Government of India—with Manmohan Singh becoming the Prime Minister in two successive governments of the UPA.

I first thanked Sonia Gandhi for her Party's leading us to our Independence but, in the same breath, mentioned that her Party was also at the root of many of our problems. I then said that her Party *had* to win the 2004 General Elections. When she asked why, I answered that Congress was the best bet to keep the secular fabric of the country intact. I, therefore, had a personal interest in her Party's—the Congress Party's—winning the elections, as that was the only Party that was capable of doing so. She then asked us how her Party could win the 2004 elections. In reply I said that the Party would need to do four things: (a) fight the elections along with like-minded Parties (which the Congress Party did); (b) accept that the Party had made mistakes in the past from which it has learnt lessons (which she admited to several times during the election campaign); (c) give the people a worthwhile programme which was precisely what we wanted to present to her (that is what the Agenda was about); and (d) convince the people that her Party would implement whatever it said in its manifesto.

I then made the presentation of the Agenda for the Nation as documented in Part II of this book. I added at the end that no one outside knew that we were there (at 10 Janpath) at that time and what the purpose of our visit was; we would like Sonia Gandhi and her Party to internalize what we had presented and treat it all as their own. The interruptions during my presentation were few and immediately taken care of by Sonia Gandhi, and I felt that we had the total attention of the audience. I may be wrong, but I did feel that there was a perceptible change in the mood in the room after we had finished our presentation. Soon after the presentation, Manmohan Singh, Jairam Ramesh, Chandana Chakrabarti, and I came out together to get into the 10 Janpath cars that take visitors to the gate. I remember the night of 29th December 2003 was specially cold, but we stood talking by the cars for half-an-hour. Jairam Ramesh said that the Party had just 100 days to do all that it should, to which I replied "That is your problem, Jairam, but if there is anything we can do we certainly will".

The next morning (on 30th December 2003) I was woken up at the Siddharth Hotel in Delhi, where Chandana and I were staying, by a call from Manmohan Singh, inviting Chandana and me for lunch at his residence on Safdarjung Road. We accepted with pleasure. There was no one else at the lunch. Manmohan Singh said that our presentation the previous evening had given his Party new hope but the Congress Party was going to lose in Andhra Pradesh to Chandrababu Naidu's Telugu Desam Party (TDP). I replied saying that if the Congress Party played its cards well (as it did), Chandrababu Naidu would not get 50 seats even in the Andhra

Pradesh State Assembly elections which were held concurrently with the General Elections to the Parliament. As it turned out, TDP did not get 50 seats in the State Assembly in the elections in 2004.

We were, after December 2003, pleased to note that there was a considerable overlap between the Agenda we had presented at 10 Janpath on 29th December 2003, the Congress Party manifesto for the 2004 General Elections, and the Common Minimum Programme (CMP) of the coalition government at New Delhi—the United Progressive Alliance (UPA)—which was led by the Congress Party and had unexpectedly won the 2004 elections hands down. We also were delighted that many of the points that we had mentioned in the Agenda were highlighted during the first address to the nation by the new Prime Minister, Manmohan Singh, after the 2004 General Elections. We, however, take no credit whatsoever for any of the above for which the credit, we feel, must go to the Congress Party and its allies that, together, constituted the UPA, and especially to those who drafted the above two documents—the Congress Party's manifesto and the Common Minimum Programme. It just shows that there have been outstanding people in the UPA and in the Parties that have supported the UPA who shared our concerns documented in the Agenda.

I attach as Annexure 1 a letter that I received from Sonia Gandhi after her Party had won the 2004 General Elections.

ANNEXURE 1 OF PART 1

(Letter dated 4th June 2004 from Sonia Gandhi to P M Bhargava)

ALL INDIA CONGRESS COMMITTEE
24, AKBAR ROAD, NEW DELHI – 110 011

Sonia Gandhi   June 04, 2004
President

Dear Shri Bhargava

I was touched to receive your kind letter.

The election result is a tribute to the strength and vibrancy of our democracy, and to the wisdom and maturity of our electorate, which has so decisively rejected the politics of divisiveness, and reaffirmed its faith in our pluralistic culture and our cherished traditions of tolerance and secularism.

I assume my responsibilities as President of the Congress Party, overwhelmed and humbled by the love and support I have received, deeply conscious of the enormous trust reposed in me, and determined to do my utmost to meet the needs and aspirations of each and every section of Indian society.

I count on everyone of you to be our guide, our critic and our conscience-keeper, so that we always remain responsive to your views and your problems, and we work together to build the India of our dreams.

With good wishes,

                                                      Yours sincerely,
                                                           Sd/-
                                                      Sonia Gandhi

Shri P M Bhargava
Furgan Cottage, 12-13-100 Lane # 1, Street # 3
Tarnaka, Hyderabad – 500 017

AN AGENDA FOR THE NATION

Expectations from the
United Progressive Alliance (UPA) Government in 2004

I. Why this Document?

As far as we are aware, as of now there is no agenda available for the nation which states the following:

- The lifestyles and the quality of life we wish to achieve
- Our assets and liabilities / problems
- The value system that is important to us
- A strategy for achieving the desired lifestyles, using our assets wisely and optimally to overcome our problems without compromising on our values. Such a strategy would require a holistic approach of networking at all levels, and not a segmented approach.

In the absence of such an agenda, our political parties spend a great deal of their time criticising each other but very little time on stating as to what they feel should be done to take the country forward. Consequently, their policies and actions are not people-oriented; they are oriented primarily towards retention of power. While we believe that many of our leaders in many political parties are well-meaning, we have felt that their concerns and abilities are not optimally utilised due to the lack of availability of an appropriate, comprehensive, people-oriented, carefully conceived and workable agenda for the nation which would enable them to focus their attention on constructive work.

Therefore, even though we are acutely aware that any agenda can at most be a torch that lights the beginning of the path, and a great deal more would need to be done to lay out the entire path and then to traverse it, we have dared to present to the nation the enclosed agenda.

The following section, Section II, states the objective of this document.

Section III describes the steps to be taken to achieve the objectives stated in the document.

Each of the seven steps mentioned in Section III to achieve the above-mentioned objectives are described in some detail in the subsequent seven sections (IV to X).

Two important areas that we have excluded from our consideration are foreign affairs and defence. We believe that policies in regard to both of these would emerge from secure and viable policies that would take care of the internal affairs of the country on which we have focussed.

II. Objective

The ultimate objective of an agenda for the nation should be to present a blueprint that would allow us

- to utilise our assets for
- overcoming our stumbling blocks—the problems—while
- operating within a framework of stated values to
- reach our defined destination in a way that is our own.

This document attempts to meet this objective.

III. Approach

We believe that to meet the objectives stated in the previous section, we must do the following:

- State the principles for defining the destination: the lifestyles and the quality of life for various sectors that we wish to achieve over a stated period (Section IV).

- Identify our assets (Section V).
- Identify the problems that the country is facing that need to be solved or overcome (Section VI).
- Establish the impact these problems have on one another to determine their hierarchy, and identify those that must be solved on a priority basis to enable the solution of other problems (Section VII).
- State the desirable values and the kind of citizens we wish to produce (Section VIII).
- Devise strategies (and network them to identify priorities) that would allow us to use our assets to take care of our problems without compromising on the stated values to reach our destination (Section IX).
- State the criteria for assessment of success (Section X).

IV. Defining Destination

A path cannot be chalked out if we have not defined the destination clearly and unambiguously. We had a vision of India when we became independent. This vision, instead of being, at most, modified to meet the demands of the changed conditions, environment and circumstances, was progressively lost sight of totally.

What, then, should be our goal or destination today, towards which all development should take us? We believe our goal should be to achieve a lifestyle for our people that would score high if measured using the yardstick for assessment of social development mentioned in Section X.

We give on pp. 35–37 the three steps that we consider important for our eventually being able to define our destination with precision.

We believe that the lifestyles envisaged would need to be different for people residing in different places, such as villages or metropolitan areas.

For example, whereas there may be a need for multi-storeyed buildings in metropolitan areas, should we encourage them in our villages? Each kind of place—and thus the lifestyle suitable for it—should offer certain specific advantages so that people have a reasonable choice.

We have classified the places for which we would need to envisage a different lifestyle in four categories: rural, tribal, semi-urban and urban. Working out in detail the desirable lifestyles for each of the above four categories would need a separate exercise. Therefore, we have stated below only the principles and the basic needs, giving examples, which are likely to act as determinants of the lifestyles for the various categories mentioned above.

Step 1: Statement of Principles

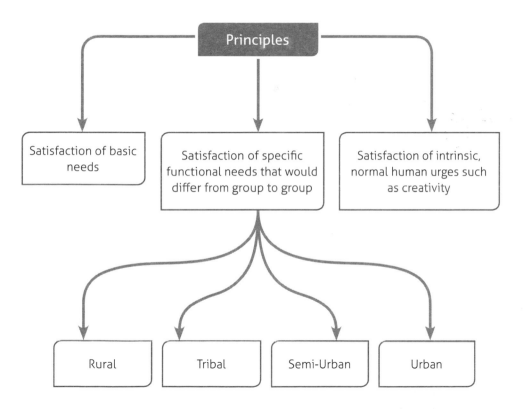

Step 2: Statement of basic and some specific functional needs of various categories of people

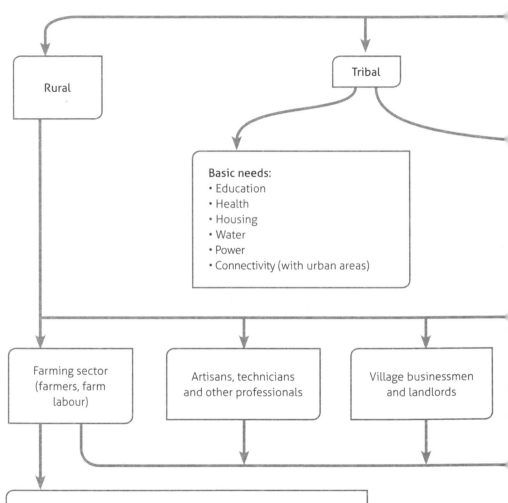

Rural

Tribal

Basic needs:
- Education
- Health
- Housing
- Water
- Power
- Connectivity (with urban areas)

Farming sector (farmers, farm labour)

Artisans, technicians and other professionals

Village businessmen and landlords

Specific functional needs:
- Additional employment avenues for farmers and their families
- Value addition to the produce of farmers
- Irrigation
- Assured and quality power
- A fair price for the farm produce
- Prevention of unfair competition from imports
- Prevention of exploitation of farm labour

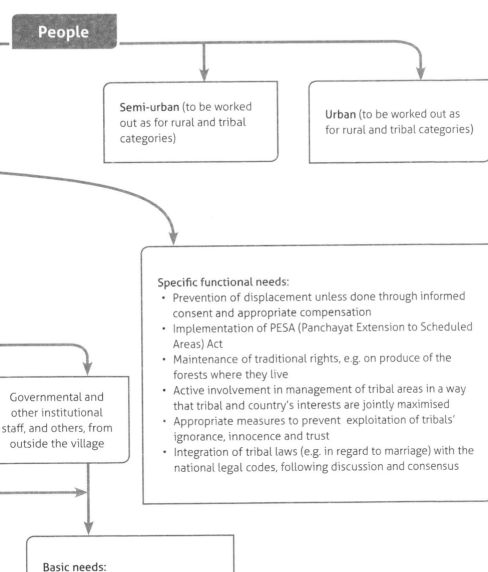

People

Semi-urban (to be worked out as for rural and tribal categories)

Urban (to be worked out as for rural and tribal categories)

Governmental and other institutional staff, and others, from outside the village

Specific functional needs:
- Prevention of displacement unless done through informed consent and appropriate compensation
- Implementation of PESA (Panchayat Extension to Scheduled Areas) Act
- Maintenance of traditional rights, e.g. on produce of the forests where they live
- Active involvement in management of tribal areas in a way that tribal and country's interests are jointly maximised
- Appropriate measures to prevent exploitation of tribals' ignorance, innocence and trust
- Integration of tribal laws (e.g. in regard to marriage) with the national legal codes, following discussion and consensus

Basic needs:
- Education • Health
- Housing • Social justice
- Water • Power
- Connectivity (with urban areas)

- Classification of people in semi-urban and urban areas into sub-groups will need to be done, as has been done here for rural or tribal areas. The basic needs as well as specific functional needs for each sub-group would need to be worked out.

- The facilities to be provided, e.g. for education, health and/or housing, for various categories and sub-groups will obviously differ from category / sub-group to category / sub-group; and would need to be worked out. For example, sources of water supply and its treatment for human consumption would be different for different categories and may depend on location; thus water tapped in situ from mountain springs may not require further treatment. Villages would not require multi-storeyed housing, unlike urban areas. Medical and healthcare facilities would also necessarily differ from category to category. Therefore, both qualitative and quantitative details (e.g. minimum residential space per person) will need to be worked out for each category and sub-group.

Step 3 : Statement of intrinsic, normal human urges such as those given below, and means of satisfying them for various categories and sub-groups mentioned above

- Creativity
- Curiosity
- Participation in community activities
- Continuous learning
- Exploration of the world beyond
  (This list is not exhaustive.)

V. Our Assets

We believe that, as of today, no other country in the world has the assets we list below. Annotations of these assets are given in Annexure 1 at the end of this part (Part II) of the book.

- Our Natural Assets
  Seven geo-climatic zones
  Vast coastline
  Water bodies
  Rainfall
  Sunlight
  Forests
  Minerals
  Land
  Animal and plant biodiversity

- Our Human Assets
  Scientific manpower
  Technological manpower
  High-level expertise in virtually all other areas of human endeavour
  Traditional and indigenous knowledge carriers
  Greatest human diversity in the world
  Large number of young people

- Our Man–Made Assets
  Science
  Technology
  Green Revolution
  White Revolution
  Information Technology revolution

Space revolution
Atomic energy revolution
DNA technology revolution
Defence technology revolution
Institution–building revolution
Drug revolution
Infrastructure in every sector

- **Our Social Assets**
  Ancient culture
  History
  Variety
  Art
  Handicrafts
  Music
  Dance
  Family set-up
  Closeness of social relations
  Social bonding
  Traditional values
  Tradition of hospitality
  Largest working democracy in the world
  Constitutional strengths

VI. Our Problems

We list below our problems in 36 categories.

1. **Governance**
   - Improper choice of peoples' representatives

- Lack of transparency and right to information
- Lack of accountability
- Lack of professionalism (e.g. in civil services)
- Inadequate electoral laws and systems
- Need to reorganise our civil services
- Inadequacies in true empowerment of our Panchayats
- Need for effective decentralisation at all levels

2. **Education**
   - Low percentage of the educated
   - Lack of appropriate education
   - Problems with curricula, syllabi, text-books, teaching methodology and assessment (e.g. misplaced emphasis on rote memory) up to high school
   - Lack of equal opportunities
   - Commercialisation
   - Unaffordability
   - Low/average quality of higher education (leading to lack of quality leaders in the next few years)

3. **Water**
   - Very little emphasis on water conservation
   - Pollution of water bodies
   - Indiscriminate and uncontrolled use of underground water
   - Emphasis on mega and long-term projects and not on local and inexpensive solutions

4. **Power**
   - Inadequate captive power generation
   - Renewable energy sources virtually untapped
   - Transmission losses and power thefts
   - Lack of a sustainable pricing policy

5. **Corruption at individual and organisational levels**
   - Readiness to pay bribes
   - Readiness to accept bribes
   - Corruption in systems such as health, education, transfers, administration

6. **Healthcare**
   - Inadequate, inaccessible and/or unaffordable primary, secondary and tertiary healthcare
   - Ineffective management of certain common diseases such as malaria, TB, AIDS and water-borne diseases
   - Inadequate and inefficient preventive health measures such as immunisation
   - Infant mortality
   - Inadequate preparedness for dealing with emerging diseases
   - Total loss of medical ethics
   - Rapidly increasing commercialisation of medical and healthcare, concurrent with increasing degeneration of such care in the public sector

7. **Sanitation**

8. **Agriculture**
   - Low productivity
   - Lack of additional employment, e.g. through food processing industry, biotechnology
   - Control of multinationals over seeds and agrochemicals
   - Excessive use of agrochemicals
   - An inefficient and inadequate public distribution system
   - Lack of use of indigenous technologies and materials
   - Organic agriculture overlooked
   - Inadequate water and power availability

9. Housing
   - How much minimum space is required?
   - What kind of housing?
   - What materials should be used?

10. Transport
   - Inadequate public transport system
   - Inadequate roads and related infrastructure
   - Inadequate planning
   - Specific transport problems
        Urban metropolitan areas
        Satellite townships
        Small urban areas
        Semi-urban areas
        Villages
        From any one of the above to the others
        Safety aspects (maintenance)

11. Justice
   - Delayed and unaffordable

12. Pollution
   - Air, water and underground

13. Deforestation

14. Environment
   - Land, air and water

15. Management and/or prevention of certain disasters
   - Flood / Drought / Famine
   - Inappropriate and ineffective relief measures and diversion of resources allotted for the purpose

- Industrial disasters
- Prevention of accidents (e.g. road, train)

16. **Employment**
    - Exploitation in unorganised sector (wages, working hours, healthcare etc.)
    - Exploitation in organised sector
    - Unemployment
    - Mal-employment
    - Child labour
    - Delinquent children in urban areas
    - Gender bias

17. **Social Security**
    - Inadequate crop insurance
    - Inadequate health insurance
    - Begging in certain parts of the country

18. **Population growth**

19. **Resource generation**
    - Lack of exploitation of the full potential of tourism
    - Inadequate efforts towards increase of productivity and provision of additional (not alternative) employment and value addition in the agricultural sector
    - No policy for prevention of wastage of products (such as primary agricultural produce) and of resources, including through corruption

20. **Group-specific problems**
    - of Tribals / Scheduled castes / Backward classes

21. **Terrorism**

22. Crime

23. Inequities
    - Regional (deliberate creation; lack of will to reassess them)
    - Sectoral (lack of a common and effective minimum wage, based on the principle of equity)
    - Inequitable (social) distribution of productive assets

24. Status of women
    - Lack of education
    - Financial dependence (even among those who earn)
    - Little role in decision-making
    - Denial of freedom of expression
    - Lack of leisure
    - Far too much labour and time spent on daily chores (e.g. collection of firewood, water)
    - Unequal pay
    - Gender-biased customs, values and attitudes (e.g. dowry, Devdasis)
    - Sexual harassment
    - Crime against women (e.g. dowry deaths and rape)
    - Physical abuse
    - Little emphasis on reproductive health
    - Inadequate nutrition
    - Bias against a girl child (e.g. in respect of nutrition and education)
    - Female foeticide and infanticide
    - Inadequate representation in public and elected bodies

25. **Lack of enough opportunities for vertical (social strata-wise/access-to-facilities-wise) and horizontal (area-wise) mobility**

26. **Lack of an appropriate scientific R & D policy**

27. Lack of proper industrial policy
    - No definition of the roles of private and public sector
    - Privatisation of public sector that is not in the national interest
    - Incursion of MNCs, including takeover of Indian companies that is destroying our autonomy

28. Lack of ethics and of national interest in the industrial sector (public and private)

29. Short-changing national interest through new patent laws, and our commitment to TRIPS and WTO

30. Lack of national commitment to values listed elsewhere (Section VIII)

31. Lack of sense of social responsibility and civic sense among individuals, in the government, and in the private sector
    - Spitting in public
    - Smoking in public
    - Easing in public (no or few public toilets)
    - Lack of cleanliness (individual, house, workplace, public place)
    - Littering
    - Inadequate garbage disposal system
    - Inadequate and/or inappropriate waste disposal (including human waste) system
    - Lack of awareness of traffic and road safety
    - Lack of awareness of problems (of village and slum dwellers) on the part of urban residents

32. Lack of accountability: social, professional and financial; individual, institutional and governmental

33. Mediocrity in all walks of life

- Lack of emphasis on excellence, professionalism and quality, leading (for example) to over 80 per cent of our graduates being unemployable

34. Lack of general awareness (of reliable and validated information) among people, e.g. in regard to the following:

- Geography (Indian and world)
- History (Indian and world)
- Nutrition (calorie, proteins, carbohydrates, fats, vitamins, essential nutrients)
- Hygiene
- Causes of diseases (water-borne, contagious, infectious, AIDS, TB, malaria)
- Creative traditions [music, art, dance, folklore, science, scriptures, literature (in one's own language and in other languages)]
- Successful people in various areas of human endeavour
- Natural phenomena and their causes (rain, weather, day and night, eclipses, earthquakes; heat, light, electricity, magnetism)
- Origin of our universe and of human being
- Customs of groups other than our own
- How products of technology work (radio, TV, telephone, mobile phone, refrigerator, heater)

35. Lack of scientific temper

- Belief in superstition, miracles, godmen, and the supernatural

36. Biases: the identity we seek

- Religious; communal
- Linguistic
- Regional
- Customs-based

- Caste and other social sub-divisions-based
- Importance of the above in choosing our friends and mate

VII. First-Level Priorities to Solve Problems

The inter-relationship of problems mentioned in the previous section, one to another, is shown in Chart 1.

Chart 1 clearly shows that our first-level priorities in regard to "problems" would be the following:
- Good governance
- Elimination of corruption
- Provision of adequate water of the required quality, depending on the use
- Making the country self-sufficient in energy so that it doesn't become limiting for development
- Provision of adequate and appropriate education

Examples of other problems, the solution of which would be dependent on the solutions to the above problems, follow on after Chart 1.

Example 1

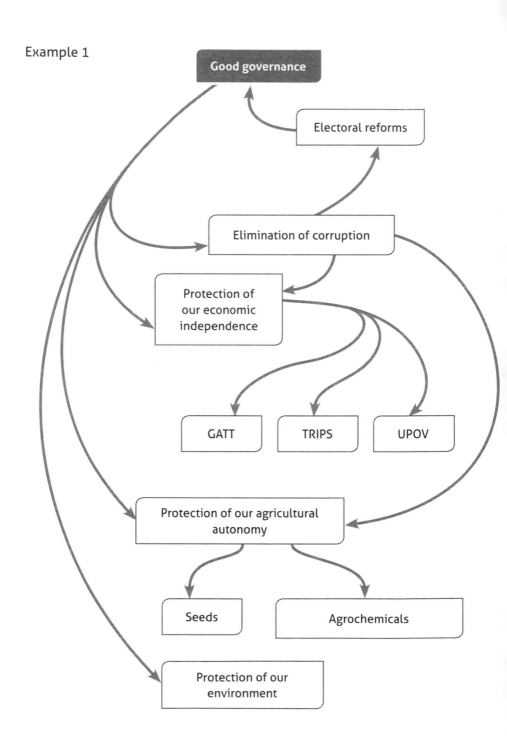

Example 2

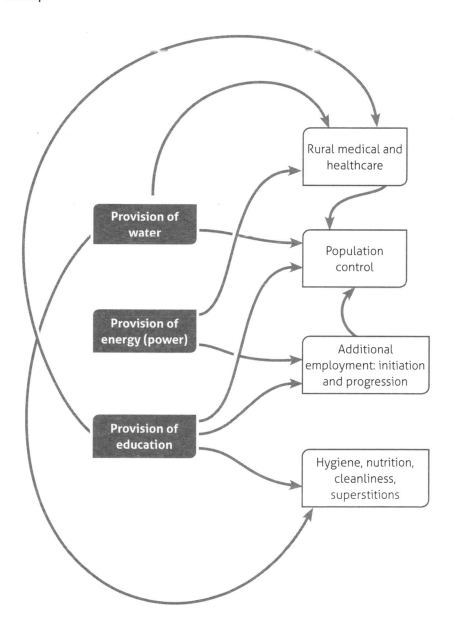

VIII. Desirable Values and Concepts and Minimal Knowledge on the Part of our Citizens

In order to define with precision the steps that we may take (Section IX) to reach the destination defined in Section IV, it is important to state what kind of citizens we wish to have, what would the values be to which we would like them to be committed, and what would the minimal knowledge be that we would like them to possess.

We state below our perception of the values that would be important for our citizens to cultivate the minimal knowledge that they should have, and the concepts of which they should have a fair understanding so that they could appreciate their implications.

1. Concept (and advantages) of a pluralistic society

2. Secularism
   - National integration
   - Equality of sexes, castes, religious groups (untouchability)
   - Internationalism
   - Interdependence of nations
   - Difference between "discrimination" and "making a distinction"
   - Impartiality

3. Concept of common good

4. Socialism and democracy
   - Understanding their implications
   - Fight against exploitation
   - Fight for social justice

5. Awareness of our Constitution

6. An understanding of the need for lasting peace at various levels

7. Commitment to UN declaration of human rights

8. Family planning

9. Cleanliness
   - Personal cleanliness (the scientific view)
   - Civic sense

10. Health and sanitation (the scientific view)

11. Balanced nutrition (the scientific view)

12. Organisation vs chaos

13. Social consciousness: advantages of social organisation

14. Team work
    - Group accomplishment
    - Cooperation
    - Networking

15. Freedom vs constraints
    - Rights and privileges vs duties and obligations
    - The right to question
    - The responsibilities associated with the right to question

16. Not to make an exception of oneself to a rule

17. Respect for others and their rights

18. Concern for problems of the future

19. Making the best use of our real accomplishments in the past, while recognising our failures during the same period.

20. Modernity
    - Contemporaneity
    - Amenability to change (acceptance of useful new knowledge and inventions, and ability to discard)

21. Efficiency
    - Ability to organise one's thoughts and actions

22. Need to work
    - Dignity of labour
    - Meaning and value of leisure

23. Commitment to excellence

24. Creative and innovative thinking
    - Healthy curiosity
    - How to find an answer to a question (the use of the method of science)

25. Relationship between education and work
    - Recognition that both are interdependent and continuing processes

26. Conservation of environment
    - Prevention of pollution
    - Understanding that the Earth is a common heritage
    - Understanding of the need for sustainable growth

27. Importance of ecology

28. Conservation of natural resources, flora, fauna

29. Prevention of waste

30. Need for understanding the environment we live in
    - Science and technology
    - Law
    - Government
    - Political systems
    - Economics
    - Planning

31. Critical attitude towards ostentation and show

32. Scientific temper
    - Objective and rational thinking
    - Clear thinking
    - Open-mindedness
    - Amenability to reason
    - Construction of viable arguments
    - Problem-solving
    - Decision-making

33. Scientific attitude towards
    - Obscurantism
    - Dogma, Irrational beliefs
    - Custom, Convention, Tradition
    - Age, Authority

34. Understanding and knowing our history and geography

35. **Aesthetics**
    - How it helps us

36. **Codes of behaviour**

37. **Personal qualities**
    - Endurance
    - Courage
    - Compassion
    - Consideration
    - Kindness
    - Helpfulness (not derived from patronage)
    - Modesty
    - Truthfulness
    - Honesty
    - Faithfulness
    - Loyalty
    - Tolerance
    - Confidence (arising out of knowledge)
    - Fairness
    - Self-discipline
    - Self-control
    - Sense of responsibility at various levels

38. **Attitude towards winning or losing in a competition**
    - Recognition of merit and excellence greater than our own

39. **Importance of**
    - Quantification and abstraction
    - Estimation
    - Accuracy

40. Recognition of the following barriers to lasting peace
   - Exploitation of the powerless by the powerful
   - Violation of basic human rights, especially of women and children
   - Lack of good and responsible governance everywhere
   - Weapons of mass destruction
   - Denial of expeditious justice
   - Religious fundamentalism and terrorism
   - Inequities
   - Corruption
   - Curbing free movement of people across national boundaries
   - Nexus between big businesses, politicians and bureaucrats
   - Inadequate water and power
   - Lack of 12 years of quality school education

Education (one of the priorities we have identified in Section VII) would clearly play an important role in ensuring that our future citizens understand the value of and are committed to the above list.

IX. The Strategy: Some Points of Action

We believe that everything mentioned in this Section is doable, and detailed, workable plans of action for each item can be provided or can easily evolve following a serious, carefully planned discussion and / or debate.

1. **Electoral reforms**
   1.1 Ensuring implementation of the 2003 Supreme Court judgement on what should be declared by any contestant for a Parliament or State Legislature seat; ensuring that no one whose honesty, integrity and probity is under doubt, or who has had a criminal case against him/her for, say, over a period is nominated by any political party for election to the Parliament or a State Legislature.

1.2   Provision of a negative vote on the ballot paper—that is, for saying that no one out of those whose names appear on the ballot paper is suitable for election.

1.3   Evolution of a mechanism for representation in important elected bodies of those who lose by a defined margin; for example, the Rajya Sabha could be made more representative from this point of view, following a constitutional amendment.

1.4   Government funding of election expenses by candidates who satisfy certain criteria; strict imposition of a ceiling on expenses, and setting up of a mechanism to ensure that the ceiling is observed.

2. Good governance

2.1   Unambiguous and workable definition of roles of MPs, MLAs, members of other elected bodies, and bureaucracy

2.2   Stoppage of grants to MPs and MLAs

2.3   Reorganisation of our civil service: professionalisation; rationalisation of recruitment policies (for example, permitting certain proportion of lateral recruitment); mid-service tests for promotion (see Annexure 2)

2.4   Decentralization (for example, reorganization of states to form smaller autonomous units, based on defined, reasonable and generally acceptable criteria)

2.5   True empowerment of local self-governments such as the Panchayats (for example, in respect of financial powers, and the powers to select and appoint the secretary of the Panchayat), making use of the extensive and admirable work done in the area by Lok Satta of Hyderabad

2.6   De facto depoliticisation of elections to Panchayats as required by our constitution

2.7   Information packages for Panchayats that would enable them to claim their rights and discharge their obligations effectively

2.8 Straightening out and computerization of land records

2.9 Providing a system for transparency in land deals and contracts, remembering that they, along with construction and building, are important conduits for corruption and black money

2.10 Establishing linkages with and making optimal use of socially sensitive, reasonable and responsible private sector, non-governmental, and professional organisations

2.11 An appropriate bill for representation of women in all public and elected bodies

2.12 Strategy for safeguarding the legitimate interests and rights of tribals, and making optimal use of their abilities and traditions (for example, in respect of conservation of biodiversity)

2.13 Ensuring that the cost of Government is less than, say, one third of the revenue generated

2.14 New strategies for raising resources for development, such as promotion of tourism, and increasing productivity and providing additional employment (e.g. through food processing, horticulture such as production and export of orchids through tissue culture in states such as Arunachal Pradesh which has over 600 varieties of exquisite and exclusively Indian orchids, and export of high quality fruits and vegetables that are virtually unique to India) in the agricultural sector

2.15 Judicious use of resources (for example, the high NPAs of banks have been largely avoidable)

2.16 Equitable regional and social distribution of productive assets

2.17 Workable and equitable system of accountability, reward and punishment

2.18 Restructuring/reorientation/consolidation of social welfare programmes for maximizing benefit to the target population

2.19 Propagation and implementation of the concept of Citizens Charter, and setting up a mechanism to ensure that the provisions of the Citizens Charters are followed

2.20 Elimination of corruption, remembering that our country was virtually corruption-free even till the 1960s (taking the first step in this direction by, for example, preparing and disseminating widely in all regional languages, a comprehensive list of corrupt practices in all sectors—governmental and non-governmental)

2.21 Appropriate legislation giving a citizen the right to information, with a clear statement of what would be classified information, why, and for how long

2.22 Setting up policies for the protection of human rights

2.23 Value-orientation in industry

2.24 Containment of the widely recognized malicious influences of multinational corporations

2.25 Planning of satellite cities and towns

2.26 Ensuring quality in services and products

2.27 Good public relations and publicity of our products and achievements round the world, for example, through our missions which have not fared well so far in this respect

2.28 Institutionalization of dissent

2.29 Regulation of disinvestments of PSUs

2.30 A viable policy for the maintenance of environment and ecology

2.31 A viable policy for balanced and sustainable growth, recognizing the crucial role of the agricultural sector in such a policy

3. Education

3.1 Schools (up to high school) to be run by local self–governments

3.2 Upgrading of all government schools to the standard of Central Schools or good, non–commercial private or public schools; revision of salaries of teachers of government schools

3.3 No transfers of school teachers (this would automatically cease if the appointments are made by the local self–governments such as the Panchayat, the Panchayat Samithi or the Zilla Parishad)

3.4 Propagation and, later, implementation of the idea of

neighbourhood schools, like the Lysees in France, for which school education would need to be decommercialised

3.5 Development of appropriate curriculae and syllabi, keeping in mind the value system to which we are committed

3.6 To improve the finances of the government–run schools; the government should be committed to provide to such schools an amount per child which should be functionally equivalent to the fees charged in good, non–commercial private schools in the area

3.7 To evolve a strategy so that schools become the focus of community activity in rural or semi–urban areas; appropriate facilities for such use of a school should be provided

3.8 A rational language policy that would recognise the role of the mother tongue as well as of English in the process of learning, in creativity, and in overall human development [while recognizing the prime importance of the mother tongue, we would not want to create in the country two classes based on the opportunity (or the lack of it) for acquiring fluency in English which is today, virtually, the international language]

3.9 Review of the examination system which, today, only tests rote memory and not understanding or knowledge

3.10 To evolve a strategy for improving the quality of higher education at universities and professional colleges (e.g., a recruitment policy that would prevent in-breeding; an independent testing organisation like the ETS in USA; and decommercialisation of higher education leading to a university degree)

4. Energy

4.1 A strategy for meeting energy requirements of the country on a time-bound basis

4.2 Energy plantations (social forestry)

4.3 Local generation of power, for example, wind power, hydel (mini and micro) power, biogas and biomass power, and solar power

4.4 Appropriate investment in research on solar power

5. Water

    5.1 Careful, objective and professional review of the project of connecting the rivers

    5.2 Rain–water harvesting (implementable strategies)

    5.3 Regulation of the use of underground water

6. Health

    6.1 Strategy for effective rural medical and healthcare: part of a three–tier strategy for national medical and healthcare, with the first two tiers (primary and secondary healthcare) being predominantly in the public sector, and the third tier (tertiary healthcare) being predominantly in the private sector (a strategy that would recognize that for the first tier, primary healthcare, we may not need medical graduates at this stage of our development, and that alternative, viable and tested models are available)

    6.2 Documentation and assessment of traditional practices, for example, in respect of plant–based drug formulations

    6.3 Formulation of a rational drug policy (for example, control of formulations and elimination of unnecessary drugs)

    6.4 Emphasis on ethics in medical practice [for example, an ethical code has been worked out by The MARCH (The Medically Aware and Responsible Citizens of Hyderabad) for hospitals, nursing homes, diagnostic centers and medical practitioners, and is being subscribed to by a substantial number of such organisations and individuals in Hyderabad, A.P.]

    6.5 Working out a more comprehensive code of medical ethics and setting up a machinery that would ensure that it is practised

    6.6 Elimination of spurious doctors (we need to state who may practise medicine, including alternate therapies) and spurious or sub-standard drugs

6.7 Setting up a centre for disease control on the lines of the Centre for Disease Control in the USA (in Atlanta, Georgia), which would be fully equipped (and having established linkages with other appropriate institutions) to identify and study new and emerging diseases

6.8 A workable strategy for waste and garbage collection and disposal all over the country

7. Increasing production and productivity in the agricultural sector

7.1 Additional employment and remunerative prices of the produce in the agricultural sector

7.2 Seed business to be made our own (Indian) to prevent foreign control of our agriculture which, if it transpires, will make us lose our freedom de facto

7.3 Strategy for self-sufficiency in food production for the growing population

7.4 Prohibition of imports that would affect the farm sector (reimposition of quantitative restrictions)

7.5 Decentralization of food procurement and distribution

7.6 Setting up a centre for animal disease control and another for plant disease control along the lines of the centre for human disease control mentioned in Section 6.7 above

7.7 Documentation, assessment and optimal utilization of indigenous agricultural practices such as organic agriculture which can be a major source of export earning [an inventory of such validated practices is available with the Indian Council of Agricultural Research (ICAR), and with Dr Anil Gupta of the Indian Institute of Management, Ahmedabad, who has also set up an organisation for this purpose]

8. An appropriate and forward-looking science and technology policy

9. International agreements and patents

9.1 A new and appropriate patent amendment bill that would safeguard our national interests (Annexure 3)

9.2 Work towards revising the provisions of WTO, TRIPS, UPOV and other international agreements that relate to trade, that severely compromise the interests of the developing countries

9.3 Full use of the existing provisions in the above agreements to our advantage

10. Defining lifestyles to optimize the effect of steps mentioned in the above nine sections

10.1 To define lifestyles for various segments of our society, as described in Section IV

[The interrelationships between action points mentioned above (except item 10) follow in Chart 2. These interrelationships reiterate the conclusion arrived at earlier that action in regard to ensuring good governance, elimination of corruption, and provision of adequate education, water and energy needs to be taken on a priority basis.]

X. Yardstick for Assessment (Indices of Social Development)

The indices described on the following pages relate—as pointed out by Prof. A K Shiva Kumar—to
- Social infrastructure
- Social awareness
- Human outcomes
- Human values

1. **Education**
   - Percentage of country's girls and boys who should be in Classes I-V, VI-VIII, IX-X, XI-XII, and who are already enrolled

2. **Availability of water**

3. **Availability of power**

4. **Health**
   - Life expectancy
   - Incidence of specific diseases (such as AIDS, TB, malaria, infestation of the GI tract with parasites) and the extent of global disease burden caused by India in relation to its population
   - Infant mortality
   - Percentage of low birth-weight babies
   - Extent of deficiency of protein, calorie, iron, vitamin A and iodine
   - Extent of disease caused by environmental factors; cancer (occupation or habit related), asbestosis, silicosis, diseases caused by non-potable water
   - Access to potable water

5. **Sanitation**

6. Corruption

- Readiness to pay bribes
- Readiness to accept bribes
- Percentage of people who do not pay any bribes

7. Status of women

- Percentage of women in government service (Class I, II, III & IV)
- Percentage of time spent by women in collection of water and preparation of food
- Percentage of women wearing a veil
- Percentage of women who need permission to go outside their houses
- Percentage of girls married below the age of 18
- Percentage of girls who have no say in choosing their husbands
- Percentage of men and women who think it is the woman's fault if she gives birth to a girl (once, twice, thrice)
- Extent of equal pay for equal work
- Percentage of those married with dowry (that is, where dowry is demanded)
- Percentage of married women suffering harassment on account of dowry matters
- Number of dowry deaths during 10-year periods, starting with 1950
- Number of rapes during 10-year periods, starting with 1950
- Percentage of marriages where dowry has been expressly declined
- Extent of sexual harassment at workplaces
- Percentage of men who don't like to have a woman as a boss
- Percentage of women who are beaten by their men
- Percentage of women who are beaten or harassed by their men— who leave their men
- Percentage of girls who should be in school but are not (Classes I–V, VI–VIII, IX–X) (Compared with the percentage of boys)
- Percentage of women going to + 2 and then degree courses (compare with a few other countries, and with men)

- Percentage of women in universities (compare with other countries and with men)
- Percentage of women in professional courses (Medicine, Agriculture, Engineering, Management)

8. Employment status
- Extent of mal-employment
- Extent of unemployment
- Number of persons in the unorganised sector as percentage of total number employed
- Percentage deriving total income from agriculture
- Extent of child labour
- Percentage of households having help under 18 years of age
- Working hours of those in unorganised sector as percentage of working hours in government or organised sectors

9. Crime record
- Extent of various crimes classified as per national crime report
- Percentage of crime that goes unreported
- Extent of child abuse

10. Economic status
- Percentage in six groups income-wise

11. General awareness about:
- Politicians
- Musicians
- Dancers
- Painters / Sculptors
- Scientists
- Industrialists
- Writers
- Academicians
- Sport Stars

- Film Stars
- Other Professionals

12. Awareness level among people about
- Knowledge of the origin of human beings
- Knowledge of the origin of the universe
- Geography (Indian, world)
- History (Indian, world)
- Nutrition (calorie, proteins, carbohydrates, fats, vitamins, essential nutrients)
- Causes of diseases (waterborne, contagious, infectious, AIDS, TB, malaria)
- Percentage of newspaper readers
- Percentage of people interested in listening to news (TV or radio)

13. Awareness of scriptures and other literature
- Literature in one's language
- Literature in any other language

14. Awareness of folk traditions
- Music, Art, Dance, Folklore

15. Awareness of customs of groups other than one's own (in age groups of 6-18, 18-40, above 40) (also, separately, in the age group of 5-10 years)
- Religion-based
- Language-based
- Caste-based
- Country-based

16. Awareness of our natural resources

17. Awareness/ knowledge of our flora and fauna and their uses

18. **Awareness of our village structure and life in our villages (to frame specific questions)**

19. **Awareness of natural phenomena and their causes**
    - Rain
    - Eclipse
    - Day and night
    - Weather

20. **Awareness of technological principles used in daily life**
    - Heater
    - Air-Conditioner
    - Refrigerator
    - Automatic toaster
    - Radio
    - TV
    - Telephone
    - Mobile phone
    - email
    - Internet

21. **Sense of social responsibility: extent of**
    - Spitting in public (especially of *pan*)
    - Throwing waste on roads and other public places
    - Smoking where prohibited
    - Disposal of waste generated in houses
    - Easing oneself in public

22. **Cleanliness: the extent and quality of cleanliness at the following levels**
    - Individual
    - House (inside/outside)
    - Workplace

23. Traffic sense: extent of
- Wearing helmets in six metros (%)
- Driving on the wrong side of roads
- Jumping traffic lights
- Faulty parking

24. Treatment of unorganised sector workers
- Percentage of people in the unorganised sector (including domestic) who treat their employees (e.g. household servants) well, i.e. in terms of pay, leave, behaviour, etc.

25. Treatment of private sector workers
- Percentage of organisations in the private sector (e.g. schools, restaurants, etc.) who treat their employees well

26. Extent of belief in the following
- Godmen
- The supernatural (e.g. the Ganesh drinking milk incident)
- Miracles
- Superstitions
- Superiority (over others) of one's religion
- Superiority of one's language
- Superiority of one's community
- Superiority of one's caste
- Superiority of one's sub-caste
- Importance of the above in choosing a mate for one's near and dear or oneself

27. Discrimination
- Extent of separate water sources, e.g. scheduled castes
- Extent to which scheduled caste members are not permitted in temples
- Appointments made on the basis of considerations other than merit

28. Percentage of friends of the

- Same religion
- Same caste
- Same sub-caste
- Same language group
- Same profession
- Not belonging to any of the above

29. What identity is sought first :

- National
- Religious
- Caste or similar sub-division
- Linguistic
- Place of origin
- As a human being

30. Leisure

- Percentage of time available for leisure among
  Students—Classes I–V, VI–VIII, IX–X; College; University
  Workers/Housewives
  Villagers—illiterate/literate/educated
  Factory workers—illiterate/literate/educated
  Lower middle class
  Upper middle class
  Upper class

- How is leisure spent
  Creative activity
  Music, dance, etc. (witnessing/performing)
  Radio/TV
  Travel
  Socialising

ANNEXURE 1 OF PART II

(Annotations for our Assets listed in Section V)

The variety in climate that you find across the world, you will also find in places across India. We are perceived to be a warm country, but we have the second coldest place (Dras in Jammu & Kashmir) in the world.

We have an extremely rich coastline of over 8000 kms.

We have an enviable network of rivers and lakes (and ponds) throughout the entire length and breadth of the country.

We receive a very substantial rainfall, with the rainiest place in the world being in our country.

We receive plenty of sunlight, and have places in the country (for example, on the coast near Tiruchendur) where there are more than 330 days of uninterrupted sunshine in a year.

We have a constitutional requirement of having one-third of the area in the country covered by forests.

We are one of the countries with the richest deposits of minerals. Our deposits of coal (including low-grade coal for the use of which we have developed processes), iron ore, mica, thorium, zinc, aluminium and oil are substantial.

We have a large land mass which is not being fully utilised.

We are one of the five regions of the largest biodiversity in the world.

We have the third largest scientific and technological manpower in the world.

There is hardly any area of technology where we do not have experts available. In areas such as custom–made software in information technology, we are among the world leaders.

We have over 40,000 distinct formulations of plant-based drugs that have come to us through five indigenous systems of medicine: the documented Ayurveda, Unani, Siddha, and Tibetian systems and the undocumented tribal systems. Even if 10 per cent of these were proven to be valid, it may exceed the equivalent number we have in modern medicine today. We have a tradition of highly innovative and useful agricultural practices, our agriculture having been contemporary with the rest of the world at the end of the 19th century, even according to a report of the British Crown at that time.

Our human biodiversity perhaps matches the human diversity across the rest of the world: we have over 450 minor ethnic groups and nearly 40 major ones.

We have, as a nation, one of the largest number (and proportion) of young people in the world today.

Our scientific and technological infrastructure is among the best in the world; we have some of the finest scientific and technological institutions in the world.

The 10 revolutions that have taken place in our country based on science and technology could be the envy of any developing country (these are: the Green Revolution, the White Revolution, the information technology revolution, the space revolution, the atomic energy revolution, the DNA technology revolution, the defence technology revolution, the institution-building revolution, the drug revolution, and the development of infrastructure in every sector). Thus, we provide the cheapest drugs in the world (many of them, such as Ranitidine for stomach problems, at less than 1 per cent of the cost at which they are available in the United States), for they have been synthesized by our creative and innovative organic chemists through routes that the original discoverers of the drugs did not envisage. For a detailed description of our successes in science and technology since Independence, and the background of these successes in our earlier history, may we refer you to our book, *The Saga of Indian Science since Independence—In a Nutshell*, published in 2003 by the Universities Press.

We are an ancient country with a documented history of nearly 5,000 years.

Our variety is unparalleled—be it in respect of religion or customs. Thus, we are the second largest Muslim country in the world, and we have more Christians than all of Australia has. Buddhism was born here, as were Sikhism and Jainism, and we have the largest number of Zoroastrians (called Parsis in India) in the world.

We have an unbroken and uninterrupted tradition of art and aesthetics, going back to 5,000 years.

Our handicrafts are unmatched anywhere.

We have two systems (the Hindustani and the Carnatic) of classical music that go back to 2,000 years, as does our tradition of dance where we have some seven (Bharatanatyam, Kuchipudi, Odissi, Kathak, Kathakali, Manipuri and Mohini Attam) classical forms of dance, all highly developed.

We greatly value family ties and social relations, and our social bonding is strong.

Our traditional values, including that of hospitality, are something which the entire world looks up to.

ANNEXURE 2 OF PART II

[An article by Pushpa M Bhargava on reorganisation of our civil services (Section IX, item 2.3), published in *The Hindu*, 23rd September, 2003]

Some two decades ago, the Education Secretary of a state government woke me up to tell me that from that morning she was Industries Secretary of the government. Education, she knew. She had a PhD in it, and she was interested and excited about it. But industry? I asked her, "How much do you know about it?" And she said truthfully, "Nothing." Unfortunately, few in her shoes would have been so truthful, for they are trained that way. But how long can we ignore the fact that, unlike 50 to 60 years ago, we are now living in an era of specialisation—with even cleaning having become highly technical.

It is for this reason that our healthcare and education (to give examples) are in shambles, in spite of the solutions to our problems in these areas staring at us. After more than 50 years of Independence, we have the largest number of the uneducated in the world, the largest number of cases of malaria and AIDS, and of polio and gastrointestinal tract infection.

We may have been better off without the National AIDS Control Organisation which has never had a top-class professional as its head. And our bureaucrats make grandiose schemes, such as linking of rivers, when far simpler and quicker solutions to the problem are at hand.

Just imagine, what the state of affairs of our space and nuclear energy programmes would have been if we had civil servants, who were transferred every few months, as Secretaries of these departments. The Department of Space of the Government of India has been, perhaps, its most successful department, and it is widely believed that the major reason for this success has been the fact that the department has had four outstanding professionals as its Secretaries: Vikram Sarabhai, Satish Dhawan, U.R. Rao and K. Kasturirangan. And our foreign service, accounts and audit service, and the railway services have done reasonably well because of having lifetime specialists to run these services.

There is, therefore, need to reorganise our civil service on the following principles:

(1). All civil service jobs must be given only to those who are specialists in the area concerned. The specialisation could be done after recruitment into the service.

(2). All appointments to a particular position in an organisation must be for at least five years with provision for extension, as is the case with secretaries of the science departments, who do not belong to the IAS or any other central service.

(3). A promotion during the five-year period should ensure that the person stays in the same organisation and the same place unless there are truly compelling reasons (such as non-performance) to shift the person.

(4). All transfers must be to a position which is in consonance with the chosen area of expertise of the individual officer.

To make the above possible, the following steps may be taken:
(i). All areas where a particular kind of expertise would be needed by the government at any given time must be identified, and then reviewed for alteration, addition, subtraction or merging every three years or so, on account of the rapidly changing structure of knowledge. Some of these areas may be economics and finance, commerce, industry, education, culture, healthcare, space, atomic energy, food and agriculture, science and technology, marine and ocean

sciences, parliamentary affairs, foreign affairs, personnel and manpower, information technology, communication, railways, roads, biotechnology, biodiversity, minerals and mining, petroleum, local self government (including Panchayati Raj), domestic affairs, land records, power, environment, forestry, electronics and automation, renewable sources of energy, tourism, civil aviation, defence, internal security, rural development, intelligence services, law, electoral process, and human rights. (This list is by no means exhaustive, or likely to be valid for all time to come.)

(ii). Applicants desirous of appearing for the IAS examination must be required to choose two or three of the areas such as those mentioned above, in order of priority. They should be tested in these areas, in addition to general knowledge and awareness, and personal and leadership qualities.

(iii). The number to be recruited in each area must be assessed every year.

(iv). The successful candidates must be posted according to the vacancies in their chosen area of first or second priority.

(v). A new incumbent in a senior position must overlap with the older one for a period of at least one month (if possible, six months) so that there is continuity. The briefing of the new person must be done over a reasonable period by the older incumbent himself or herself and not by the staff down the line after the older incumbent has left.

(vi). There must be provision of lateral recruitment of top-class and experienced professionals into the service—say up to 25 per cent of the positions, depending on the need and availability of such persons.

Already, an increasing number of professionally trained individuals are joining our civil service. The above steps would ensure the optimal utilisation of the immense talent we continue to have in our civil service—particularly in view of the continuously decreasing breadth and depth of knowledge among our politicians to whom our bureaucrats report.

ANNEXURE 3 OF PART II

[An article by Pushpa M Bhargava on safeguarding our interests in
our patents bill (Section IX, item 9.1),
published in *The Hindu,* 20th February, 2002]

The suggestions that follow for inclusion in the new patents bill before Parliament are based on (a) recognition of the fact that many provisions of TRIPS are weighted heavily in favour of the developed countries; (b) that there are provisions in TRIPS that can be used to maximise and protect our national interests; and (c) that the decisions taken at the WTO's Doha meeting provide for even greater flexibility in the use of certain provisions of TRIPS that would be in our interest provided we have the wit and the courage to use these provisions. An example of maximising the protection of our interests is the recent Plant Varieties Protection Act passed by Parliament. Although some provisions of this Act could be improved upon, by and large it would help our farmers and thus also help protect our agriculture.

The following are some of the problems with TRIPS:

Article 23 (Additional Protection for Geographical Indicators for Wines and Spirits) when we have Article 22 (Protection of Geographical Indicators).

Article 27.1 which permits patenting of products, not recognising that the development of an alternative process for the production of, say, a drug, is as much of an intellectual challenge as developing a new product to begin with.

Article 27.3(b) which permits patenting of microorganisms (naturally occurring or genetically engineered).

Article 31 about compulsory licensing in which terms such as "reasonable" and "adequate" have been used without definition.

Article 34 which puts the burden of proof on the defendant.

Some suggestions for inclusion in the new patents bill are given below. The bill must provide for protection of our geographical indicators such as various kinds of Indian tea, basmati and other rice indigenous to India, the many varieties of Indian mangoes, the orchids found only in the Himalayas (which would include several hundred varieties found only in Arunachal Pradesh), and so on. It must state that any derivatives of Indian geographical indicators based on the germplasm of these indicators would not be patentable. This may not mean very much for us but it will prevent the use of our market by people who may, for example, use basmati rice as a starting material for developing a new variety with minor genetic modifications. We should recognise that India would eventually be one of the world's largest markets.

We could use the provisions of Article 27.2 and Articles 8.1 and 8.2 to take care of some of the problems that would arise following implementation of Article 27.1. One suggestion would be to include a clause in the patents bill that the government will set up a high-power committee which would, say, every six months, prepare a list of products (including drugs) for which cheaper alternatives than the patented one are available in India through the efforts of our scientists such as organic chemists, and the production of which through the new process would make it cheap enough to be within the reach of the masses, and thus necessary "to protect order public or morality, or human, animal or plant life or health, or to avoid serious prejudice to the environment". The committee will then permit, using the above quoted provision under Article 27.2 and similar provisions under Articles 8.1 and 8.2, the production of these products by the new process in the country even though the product (made by another process) may have been patented by a party outside the country. To make optimal use of the provisions under Article 27.3(a), we must clearly spell out that no chemical entity (such as a monoclonal antibody) that is used for diagnosis or for preparing diagnostic kits, and no diagnostic kit or product would be patentable.

As regards Article 27.3(b) of TRIPS, our patent law must exclude patenting of naturally occurring or genetically engineered plants, animals and microorganisms (including those of marine origin) or any product(s) derived from them. In the case of such products, their patenting may be permissible only if a new use has been found for them which has not so far been known to humanity, either through published literature or through tradition. The amendment must also clearly state that naturally occurring genes, single nucleotide polymorphisms (SNPs), and naturally occurring macromolecules such as DNA will not be permitted to be patented.

We may permit the patenting of a specified process for producing a genetically engineered plant, animal or microorganism using a specified starting organism. Thus, we may permit the patenting of a new process for producing a transgenic sheep of a certain breed, designed to produce a specific protein in a specified organ or secretion (such as milk), made by a specified procedure in which every element that is used (such as the vector) is defined.

The new patents bill must cover all Indian traditional plant-based medical formulations (estimated to be about 40,000) that are part of either the documented Ayurveda, Unani, Siddha or Tibetan systems of medicine or the undocumented tribal systems of medicine, or which can be demonstrated to be part of our culture and for which social, if not, written validation exists. Thus the use of any of these formulations, or any modified versions of them, for any disease which can be identified with symptoms for which the formulations have been traditionally used, would not be patentable. A use patent could be granted for even a known formulation or a modification of it, if it has been shown to be useful for purposes for which it has never been used early. An example would be the two patents of Baruch Blumberg (a Nobel prize-winning scientist who discovered the Hepatitis B virus) on a preparation of *phyllanthus amarus* which has been widely used all over India (and elsewhere) for curing symptoms that correspond to Hepatitis B; these patents cannot be challenged as he has shown that the drug inhibits two key enzymes of the virus and actually clears the Hepatitis B virus from carriers. Similarly, patents should be grantable for developing processes for stabilisation of a traditional formulation so that it becomes commercially marketable. However, changes in the methods of extraction for a traditional medical formulation must not be permitted to be patented.

As regards Article 31, we should clearly state that compulsory licensing would be automatic if three years have lapsed after the grant of the patent or five years after the filing of the patent, whichever is less, and the person or party desirous of producing the product in India has written to the patentee and received no reply within 90 days of proof of delivery of the communication to the patentee. As regards Article 34, we must insist that in the case of an alleged violation of a patent, the burden of proof would lie on the owner of the patent and not the defendant. We must also not permit patenting of formulations, drug metabolites, particle size variants and polymorphs.

SUCCESSES AND FAILURES

OF THE UPA GOVERNMENT BETWEEN 2004 AND 2012

As the following review will show, out of 72 items listed for action under 10 sub-sections in Section IX of the Agenda for the Nation (Part II of this book), some concrete or effective action has been taken by the UPA Government between 2004 and 2012 only in regard to six items (the numbers below refer to numbers in Section IX of Part II of this book).

1.   Electoral reforms

1.1   **Recommendation:** "Ensuring implementation of the 2003 Supreme Court judgement on what should be declared by any contestant for a Parliament or State Legislature seat; ensuring that no one whose honesty, integrity and probity is under doubt, or who has had a criminal record (or a criminal case against him/her for over a year), is nominated by any political party for election to the Parliament or State Legislature."

Action taken: Implemented only to the extent of having formal declarations made by candidates, which declarations also are often incorrect. We continue to have people who are in jail contest elections, and we continue to have people in our Parliament, State Assemblies and other elected bodies, whose honesty, integrity and probity has been under serious doubt.

Comment: Action taken is far from adequate.

Note added in proof: **Action taken on Recommendation 1.2:** The option for Indian voters to choose None of the Above (NOTA) has been added to the ballot in 2013. Although it gives the right to register a negative opinion, it does not translate into "the right to reject" all candidates. Even if maximum number of voters press the NOTA button, the election will be decided in favour of the candidate who gets the maximum of the remaining votes.

(*No action taken on the other two recommendations under Electoral Reforms.*)

2. Good governance

2.8   **Recommendation**: "Straightening out and computerization of land records".

Action taken: While this has been done in some states (for example, in West Bengal and Kerala by non-Congress governments), unfortunately, it remains to be done in most of the states.

Comment: A lot yet remains to be done.

2.12   **Recommendation:** "Strategy for safeguarding the legitimate interests and rights of tribals, and making optimal use of their abilities and traditions (for example, in respect of conservation of biodiversity)."

Action taken: The UPA Government has passed an Act protecting the rights of forest dwellers (tribals) but none of the provisions of this Act have been actually implemented. Even the earlier Act, PESA, which pertained to governance in tribal areas, has not been implemented.

Comment: The UPA Government has failed totally.

2.21   **Recommendation:** "Appropriate legislation giving a citizen the right to information, with a clear statement of what would be classified information, why and for how long".

Action taken: The UPA Government has done very well in passing the Right to Information Act which has been one of its most celebrated successes. It may, however, be recalled that this Act was not passed at the initiative of the Government but at the initiative of civil society.

Comment: This is one action of the UPA for which it must be congratulated.

2.30 Recommendation: "A viable policy for the maintenance of environment and ecology".

Action taken: Although we still do not have a viable policy for the maintenance of environment, ecology and biodiversity, Jairam Ramesh, former Minister for Environment and Forests, took certain admirable decisions in the above areas which, in the present environment, required courage. One of them was the indefinite moratorium on the open release of genetically modified Bt-brinjal.

Comment: It is yet to be seen whether the traditions set up by Jairam Ramesh continue to be maintained.

(*No action taken on the 27 other recommendations under Good Governance.*)

---

3. Education

Comment: *None of the ten recommendations made have been followed.* The Right to Education Act which should have taken care of item 3.2 (upgrading of government schools) was widely considered unimplementable when it was passed a couple of years ago. As it turns out, not one of the provision of this Act has been implemented so far. The same is true of item 3.10 (improving the quality of our higher education). We have an excellent report on how to do this prepared by the Yashpal Committee but there seems to be no desire on the part of the UPA Government to implement this report. In this context, we are attaching an article (Annexure 1) written by one of us in the *Economic and Political Weekly* that also states the steps that might be taken to improve the quality of our higher (including professional) education and to universalize access to it. Many of the recommendations made in this article, which was written before the Yashpal Committee submitted its report, are included in the Yashpal Committee Report.

4. Energy

Comment: *None of the four recommendations made have been followed.* On the other hand, there has been unwarranted emphasis on nuclear energy which, if pursued in India, would bring much greater benefit to the US (and other countries) than to India. For our country, over-emphasis on it may even be disastrous, specially when we have alternatives right before our eyes.

5. Water

Comment: *None of the three recommendations made have been followed.* On the other hand, the UPA Government seems to be inclined to privatize water which would severely aggravate the water problem for a vast majority of our citizens.

6. Health

Comment: *None of the eight recommendations made have been followed.* There is an excellent report of a group headed by Srinath Reddy that would take care of many of the health problems in the country, but the UPA Government does not seem to be inclined to implement this report's recommendations.

7. Increasing production and productivity in the agricultural sector

Comment: *None of the seven recommendations made have been followed.* Annexure 2 (an article by one of us on Agriculture Security, published in *Social Change*) outlines in some detail several important steps that we may take to ensure agriculture security, food security, farmers security and, thereby, security of the rural sector. None of these steps has been taken so far.

8. **An appropriate and forward-looking science and technology policy**

   Comment: *No such policy statements have been made by the UPA Government*, in spite of the fact that science and technology have become increasingly intermeshed with the very fabric of our society.

9. **International agreements and patents**

   9.1 **Recommendation:** "New and appropriate patent amendment bill that would safeguard our national interests (see Annexure 3 of Part II)"

   Action taken: The UPA Government has passed a Patent Amendment Bill that has taken care of some of the problems mentioned in Annexure 3 of Part II of this book.

   Comment: However, several of the lacunae in the TRIPS and other related international agreements that we have signed, remain. *(No action taken in regard to the two other recommendations in Section 9 of Part II of this book.)*

10. **Defining lifestyles to optimize the effect of steps mentioned in the above nine sections**

   Comment: *Nothing has been done by the UPA Government in this direction.*

ANNEXURE 1 OF PART III

(An article by Pushpa M Bhargava on revamping higher education, published in the *Economic and Political Weekly*, July 21-27, 2007, pp. 3060-3063. It refers to item 3.10 in Section IX of Part II, and comments on this item in Part III of this book)

The recommendations of the National Knowledge Commission (NKC) on higher education, which were recently discussed in the *Economic and Political Weekly* of February 17 and March 10, 2007, were sent to the Prime Minister in spite of my repeatedly writing to the Chairman—as a member (Vice-Chairman) of the NKC—that they needed to be further discussed. It was only on 19th December 2006 that I learnt through a press report in a Delhi newspaper that these recommendations had been sent to the Prime Minister on 29th November 2006.

As the Prime Minister rightly stated when the above-mentioned recommendations on higher education were presented to him in person, along with some other recommendations, by the Chairman of NKC on 12th January 2007 that these recommendations should be debated in the country before finalization. As a part of this debate, I am presenting here a list of possible action points in regard to higher education that may be able to address some of the problems we have in the country today in this important area. As these problems, relating (for example) to purpose of higher education, access to it (who gets in and how), the nature and number of universities we need (the problem of "quantity"), and quality (of teachers, infrastructure, management and governance), are well-known, they are not stated in any detail; only some steps that could be taken to at least partly take care of the problems are indicated. The list presented is by no means exhaustive; it is only indicative and is presented here for debate. The suggestion given here have only a small overlap with the recommendations of the NKC mentioned above; they differ from the latter in many vital respects.

I have assumed that we should plan for 20% of eligible students to go for higher education. It is further assumed that a university with only a few hundred students on the roll is not a viable proposition. The average optimal size of a university is taken to be 10,000 students including those going for a professional degree, say in medicine, agriculture, engineering or law.

Pre-requisites

No matter what we do, we cannot take care of higher education appropriately and adequately unless we take care of school education: unless we ensure that every child in the country in the age group of 6 to 18 has equal access to high-quality education from Class I to Class XII (to begin with, perhaps, to class X), which can happen only by decommercialising school education and adopting a common (neighbourhood) school system, with private (de facto and de jure not-for-profit) schools being a part of it. We need 4,00,000 higher secondary schools of the quality of our Central Schools, funded by the Central/State Government but run by the local self government and civil society. When all the above happens in respect of school education, we would not need any reservation in higher education, and would be optimally utilizing our gene pool—of which, today we are not using more than five per cent!

We must also recognise that, concurrently with taking care of our school education, we must take care of quality vocational education and training at various levels with multiple entry and exit points, with some of the exit points routing one towards university education. We need to expand the number of vocational training institutes from today's 5,000 to 50,000 to begin with and later, 2,00,000. We need to provide vocational training in not just 80 or so vocations as we are doing today, but in at least several hundred, including traditional vocations such as weaving and metal work.

It is only when we have put appropriate systems for school and vocational education in place that we can hope to solve our problems of higher education on a long-term basis. However, a beginning can be made with the suggestions that follow that may provide a viable framework for change.

Objective of Higher Education

If higher education is in a professional course then the objective should clearly be to prepare a person for a profession. This would be true also of vocational education at all levels. However, the objective of university education in basic disciplines, such as physics, chemistry, sociology, economics, biology, history or languages, should be to produce experts in the area who are knowledgeable and excited about the field, and who are capable of engaging in research to push the frontiers of knowledge, or in creative or productive activities that would be related to their field; the culture of such university education should provide them with an excellent starting point for their chosen pursuit. Such people, if they turn out to be true experts in the field, would rarely be without a job; history shows that for such people jobs are created and that is how knowledge advances.

There should be a substantial investment in higher education (ideally, 1.5 per cent of GDP which should be possible when the government fulfils its commitment to provide 6 per cent of GDP for education). While private institutions granting degrees should be encouraged, it should be ensured by a suitable legislation (an Act of the Parliament) that they are de facto and de jure not commercial institutions (that is, like companies). All profit made by such institutions should be ploughed back to meet the objectives of the institutions within the country. They should be set up following the same procedure as a publicly-funded institution, and they should submit themselves to the same regulatory mechanism as the publicly-funded institutions.

No Foreign Educational Providers (FEPs) should be allowed to set up educational facilities in India for profit which would not be entirely ploughed back into the institution in India but used to support the parent institution abroad, or accrue to an individual or individuals as to share holders in profit-making companies. Only a well-known foreign institution (say, among the top 200 universities in the world) may be allowed to set up campuses here, solely following an altruistic motive. Such institutions must give an Indian degree and be subject to all rules and regulations that would apply to a wholly Indian university.

There should be no bar to private for-profit organizations in the technical sector that provide specific training in an area of interest to the country and its people; they should not be authorized to provide a degree (but can provide a diploma or a certificate), and must operate ethically. They should be regulated by a separate authority that will ensure, through appropriate mechanisms (such as a security deposit with the government), that the students are not taken for a ride and get an appropriate return on their investment.

Choices
The choices that a student passing (or not passing!) high school may have are best stated diagrammatically (Figure 1).

Access
   (i).   Admission must be means blind and made on the basis of merit
          and not on the basis of a student's ability to pay—be it in private
          or in state-run universities.
  (ii).   Poor students must be supported financially and schemes
          must be worked out for this, including bank loans, following an
          arrangement between a bank and the university.
 (iii).   In principle, every student's fee should be paid, be it by the
          student (through one's own resource or through a university–
          arranged bank loan), by the State, or by the university (through
          scholarships).

How may students get in?
   (i).   There should be a national test like that conducted by
          Educational Testing Services (ETS) of Princeton, but testing both
          scholastic ability as well as social experience and sensitivity, for

admission to a university, which the students should take during the last year of their +2 course.

(ii). The test should be conducted, say, six times a year (if not every month), and a student should be able to take the test as many times s/he wishes, and ask for any test score to be sent or not to be sent to the universities of his choice.

(iii). There should be a nominal fee for the test. While registering for the test, the student should give preferences of universities all over the country. The universities can then decide whom to take on the basis of the test score.

(iv). If a person has succeeded in obtaining admission to more than one university, he or she must indicate by, say, January, the university of his or her preference—so that all universities finalise their admissions by, say May. All this can be done easily using information and communication technology (ICT).

(v). The above test should cover all private universities too.

(vi). It is recognised that once every child in the country is in a position to go up to Class XII (that is, the Intermediate College of today), and have his/her education in an excellent institution (like the Central Schools of today), there would be no need for reservations based on any criterion of social backwardness or deprivation in higher education. Till that time, we would clearly need to have reservation for intrinsically meritorious but socially deprived or backward children whose environment has not provided them adequate opportunities for expression of merit to the extent that the system of selection for admission to higher educational institutions may demand. For this purpose, a social deprivation index that takes into account various factors should be worked out by an expert group. This index could, for example, have a rating of 1-20 marks out of a total of a 100 that a student may get in any assessment system for admission to a university. The marks obtained following the use of this index should be added to the other marks obtained by the student. For such a system to work, an extreme penalty will need to be imposed for any deliberate misinformation provided by the student for determination of the social deprivation index. This index should be determined by organisations that may conduct the national tests mentioned earlier for admission into universities and added to the marks obtained by the student in the regular test. As mentioned above, the social deprivation index should account for up to 20 per cent of the total marks.

Quantity
We need 3,000 good universities (that is, universities which satisfy all the criteria laid down by the Higher Education Regulatory Authority mentioned later), each with not more than 10,000 students. This can be achieved in the following way:
  (a) Upgrade existing (nearly 300) universities by, for example, providing a certain percentage of their budget as an extra grant every year, after ensuring that they follow the new norms of the Higher Education Regulatory Authority mentioned later.
  (b) Set up new universities, to begin with, perhaps 20, in the next five years.
  (c) Convert good colleges (out of the over 17,500 we have) that satisfy criteria laid down by the Higher Education Regulatory Authority (mentioned later) into universities—private or State-run—ensuring that they are not (de facto or de jure) commercial institutions set up to make profit for individuals. They must be provided an additional grant to make up deficiencies, if any, specially in the area of research.
  (d) Small colleges in a city, that are good and are not de facto or de jure commercial institutions, could together, similarly, form a university in which, for example, the faculty would be transferable from one constituent college to another; one college could have one department and another college another department.

The remaining affiliated colleges may be given three options: (i) to convert into trade-related institutions training people for specified vocations / trade; (ii) to upgrade within five years to a level that would enable them to be given an autonomous university status (to wind up within the subsequent two years, if this does not happen in the first five years); or (iii) to wind up within a reasonable time (not more than five years), with no new admissions from the following year.

It should be noted that no country in the world has the extensive system of affiliated colleges we have. Few of the over 17,500 affiliated colleges are capable of doing any worthwhile research or even employ outstanding academicians. The students are, therefore, as a rule, denied the latest in terms of knowledge imparted by the best of minds, besides the advantages of a university culture. A large proportion of them produce unemployable graduates. It is, therefore, not surprising that, as Kiran Karnik, Chairman of National Association of Software and Services Companies (NASSCOM), says, over 70 per cent of our engineering graduates are unemployable. Further, the existence of affiliated colleges has had many of our universities stop having undergraduate classes! Thus, none of the 13 universities in Andhra Pradesh have undergraduate classes. Compare this situation with that in, say, the US and the UK (or elsewhere) where it may be difficult to find a university that does not have undergraduate classes on its own campus.

Employment
Employers may conduct their own tests to ascertain suitability of the output of the university system.

Quality: Teachers, Infrastructure, Management and Governance
Set up a Higher Education Regulatory Authority (HERA) which will perform the following functions:
   a) Grant licence to give degrees.
   b) Set up quality benchmarks and lay down standards.

c) Licence assessment agencies both in the public and the private sectors.
d) License agency for assessment of students wishing to enter the portals of a university.
e) Be responsible for disbursement of government funds, and set up transparent and objective criteria and mechanism for that purpose.
f) Grant licence to practise various professions after obtaining a professional degree.

The function of organisations such as the National Accreditation & Assessment Council, University Grants Commission (UGC), All-India Council of Technical Education, (AICTE), the Medical Council of India, the Pharmacy Council of India, and the Bar Council, will then need to be redefined. They—one or more of them—could act as agencies that would assess universities, or provide grants to universities, on behalf of HERA. Functions such as giving of grants or running of refresher courses could be performed autonomously by these agencies after they have been appropriately restructured.

HERA should consist of a Chairman, a Vice-Chairman and eight to ten other members, some of whom could be part-time. All the members of HERA should be top-class academicians with high public creditability and integrity, and known commitment to fairness and objectivity. They should have a demonstrated interest in education and a wide vision, and be articulate and receptive to others' ideas, besides having established managerial qualities. HERA must be autonomous (both de facto and de jure) and free of political interference. It must establish channels of quick communication with the academic community of the country. Its composition, detailed structure and mode of functioning must be designed through a national debate and consensus to ensure that it does not go the same way as its predecessors.

HERA should be complemented by similar State Higher Education Regulatory Authorities to whom HERA could delegate a part of its responsibilities under a specified set of conditions. A major responsibility of HERA would be to ensure implementation of the other provisions of this article or additions to (and subtraction from) them from time to time. It should be ensured by setting up a suitable system of accountability and transparency that HERA does not come to suffer from the same problems that existing organisations such as the ones mentioned above are widely known to suffer from.

Some of the other steps we may take are:
- Institute a new stringent, objective and fair system of appointment of university teachers. All university appointments should be open to all citizens of the country, and some (a designated) proportion even to people from other countries. Introduce transparency and accountability in regard to above.
- Increase proportion of non-tenure, contract appointments.
- Prevent inbreeding by suitable conventions. (Today, inbreeding is the rule in a vast majority of our universities.)
- Remove barriers to involving appropriate people from outside India in teaching and assessment at various levels.
- Make retirement age flexible for outstanding academicians that satisfy specifically laid down stringent criteria.
- Make provision of compulsory retirement with full benefits for non-performers of today—till the new system takes root.
- Bring back undergraduate courses to all universities that do not have them.
- Set up a code (through HERA) for university teachers, say in regard to attendance, number of teaching hours, and the teacher-student ratio. The most famous and the best-known members of the faculty should teach undergraduates, as is customary around the world.

- Dissociate salary from position and function in the academic world (examples are available).
- Provide liberal (not time-bound) incentives (such as an increase in salary) for proven and recognised accomplishments of university teachers. (Some suggestions follow later.)
- Abrogate existing system of time-bound promotions. Link career prospects for the staff of academic institutions with performance evaluated stringently.
- Set up a stringent (but a transparent, fair and objective) system of continuous evaluation of institutions based on specific but dynamic criteria. (This system should be set up by HERA.)
- Introduce salary differentials (within a specified range) within a department, within a university, and between universities, to attract talent in areas of high demand.
- Make provision for regular part-time employment (e.g. one could have two half-time secretaries instead of one full-time, or a university teacher could draw part of his / her salary from the university and part from an industry). Thus, encourage multi-institutional affiliation of academics (including public-private mix).
- Encourage multiple appointments for outstanding academicians (e.g. in a university and a research lab, or an Indian university and a foreign university, or a university and an industry). Frame appropriate rules that would encourage consultancy.
- Evolve a system of evaluation of teachers by students.
- Set up a system to ensure that every university has appropriate infrastructure facilities that are adequately professionalised (examples would be: workshop, instrument repair, dispensary, bank, cleaning, security). A list of some 60 such "tested" facilities is available with us.
- Abolish over a period of 10 years all affiliated colleges in all areas (including professional ones).

- Revise procedure for selection of vice-chancellors so that the decision is made by the academic community / chancellor without any political interference of any kind.
- Restructure management of universities to decentralize power and decision-making, and encourage collegiate management. Minimise the roles of V-C, Registrar, and Head of Department (HOD). Change the system of rotation of HODs. Make compartmentation into "department" or "faculty" or "schools" dynamic instead of being rigid, and create "virtual departments" to represent emerging areas of knowledge.
- Adopt fully (not partially) course and credit system (on the lines of what is obtained in the US) in universities, thus changing the examination system entirely to internal assessment as is, for example, obtained in the US. Provide flexibility so that a student can complete the requirements for a degree in any period s/he wishes. Thus an indigent student can work part-time and complete a degree in, say, five years instead of the minimum of three years. Contents of the course should be determined by the teacher but the outline should be included in the information booklet of the university to be published every year, a year in advance, and put on the university's website which every university must set up.
- Ensure that research publications (articles, journals) from the country adopt the open access system to the maximum possible extent.
- Encourage the use of open source software.
- Revise procedure for PhD examination. For example, have at least one examiner from one of the, say, 500 best universities and research institutions abroad; the viva could be conducted through a conference call.
- It should be recognised that in a university some people are excellent teachers but not outstanding research workers while there are others who are outstanding research workers but not good teachers. This should be kept in mind when distributing the

teaching load in a university. Teachers should teach a course over a semester during which they may not be normally permitted to absent themselves from their teaching duties for any reason whatsoever and irrespective of their status, as is the practice in reputed institutions all over the world. A system should be set up for international assessment of every university once in, say, every ten years. This should be done by people of undisputed academic and/or professional ability, interest in India, lack of any bias, and commitment to a high level of excellence.

- Change the accounting systems of academic and research organisations to increase accountability (professional, social and financial), with no interference in academic matters. The Comptroller & Auditor General (CAG) has, for example, a separate cell for auditing certain science departments.
- Set up an ICT-based system for maximising national benefit from the visit of foreign visitors that are often invited by one organisation.
- Remove fragmentation of education (e.g., as of today, medical and agricultural colleges are often under ministries of health and agriculture with no coordination with education ministries, and their staff is subject to unwarranted transfers that preclude their doing any research).
- Set up a system of interaction with civil society to elicit their involvement. This could be done, for example, by offering extra-mural courses to members of the public—say, in the evening—and having public lectures.

Finances

- As mentioned above, the government should work towards having 1.5 per cent of the GDP allocated for higher education.
- All universities should be encouraged to create a corpus fund and assets through investment. They should be permitted to

engage the services of investment managers as is the case with many universities outside the country. The professional management of assets over a period can generate substantial wealth. Under no circumstances, should the permanent immovable assets of the university, such as land, be sold or alienated on a de facto permanent basis.

- The universities should also employ professional fund raisers who should be able to identify the unique selling points of the university and persuade, for example, private donors to donate money to the university. One impediment today in this endeavour is the lack of any trust on the part of a potential donor that the money given to the university would be appropriately utilized. The university must, therefore, create an environment of transparency and of commitment to excellence which would persuade donors to support the university. In addition, it must have overhead charges built into research proposals. Provision of various services and licensing of patents could be other sources of revenue. No deduction must be made from the governmental grant to a university following its success in raising funds from elsewhere. In fact, for say 10 years, the government should provide financial rewards to universities that raise their own funds which would be in addition to the normal grant by the government to the university: something like the weighted tax deduction for research and development in industries.

Figure 1

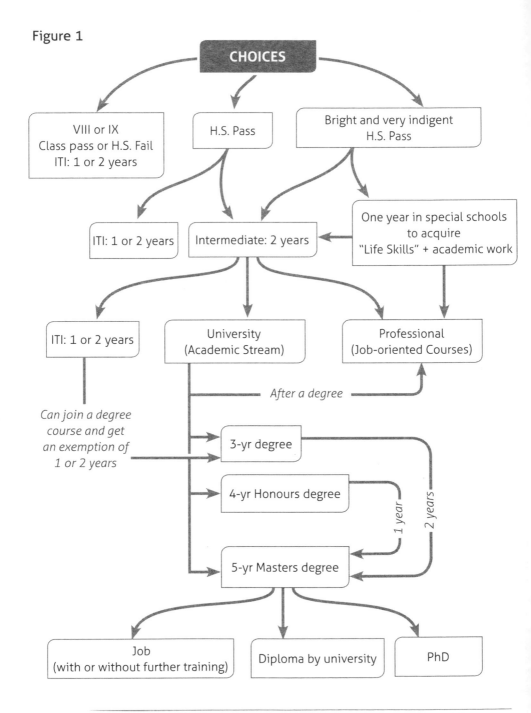

Note: ITI means an Industrial Training Institute or a similar vocational training centre

ANNEXURE 2 OF PART III

(An article by Pushpa M Bhargava on how to achieve agriculture
security, published in *Social Change,* March 2008, pp. 1-30. It refers
to item 7 of Section IX of Part II, and comments on this item in
Part III of this book)

SUMMARY

This article emphasises the virtual synonymity of agriculture security, food security, farmers' security, and security of the rural sector, and the importance of ensuring the above to ensure national security.

Operationally, the following components of agriculture security have been identified:
seeds; agrochemicals; water and power; soil; agricultural practices (traditional and modern); de juro/de facto empowerment of Panchayats; marketing of agro-products at fair/remunerative prices; other sources of augmentation of income of agriculturists and village dwellers (such as traditional arts and crafts, medicinal plants, plants producing biodiesel, fruits and vegetables, organic farming, post-harvest technologies, intelligent energy use, animal husbandry, fisheries and marine wealth, and orchid tissue culture); knowledge empowerment of rural sector (both long-term through formal school education, and short-term through knowledge packages for Panchayats); loans, e.g. through microcredit; integration of rural and urban sectors, e.g. through roads, communication, appropriate industry, and medical and healthcare; policy, e.g. effective administration of NREGS; research and extension; external threats; disasters such as flood and famine; cultivable land and land records; bioterrorism; rare, emerging, new and exotic diseases of plants and animals, and climate change.

The current problems the country is facing in each of the above areas are defined and concrete steps suggested to take care of them.

It is recommended that a high-power apex body chaired by the Agriculture Minister should be set up to examine in detail the above recommendations and work out mechanisms to implement those that are found to be worthy of implementation. One of the functions of the proposed apex body should be to put together every year reliable data on the production (and productivity, for example per person, per animal, per unit land, or per rupee spent, as appropriate) as well as consumption per person, of cereals, pulses, fruits, vegetables, milk, poultry, marine food, and meat.

I. The Crisis

Food security, important for every country, means ensuring availability of enough food for the people of a country at affordable prices that would take care of the basic nutritional requirement of the population on a sustainable basis. There are two ways of ensuring food security:
(a). dependence primarily on indigenous production; or
(b). dependence primarily on imports against exports of other indigenous products to countries that cannot do without receiving such exports.

For India, the first alternative is clearly the one of choice as a vast majority of our population (over 60 per cent) is engaged in agriculture, and some 70 per cent of our people derive their total income from agriculture or agriculture-related activities such as animal husbandry and fisheries, or activities in the rural sector that support our agriculturists. Therefore, agriculture security in our country should be considered functionally synonymous with food security, and with the security of our farmers and of the rural sector where they live and work.

Given this perspective, India's agriculture security is facing a serious crisis as is clear from the following:
(a). From a situation of self-sufficiency in food following the Green Revolution in the 1960s, we now need to import five million tons of wheat alone this year, besides other food items such as vegetable

oil, without a corresponding increase in the export of agro-products; and this is not the first year we would be doing so.

(b). Virtually no attention has been paid to the plight of small farmers (with holdings of 2 to 4 hectares) and marginal farmers (with less than 2 hectares who account for 84% of our farmers).

(c). Suicides by farmers continue unabated. Some 40 per cent of farmers, even though in love with their land, want to opt out of farming as a profession. There has been, thus, a substantial migration from the villages to the cities which have been ill-equipped to handle this migration in any civilized manner.

(d). Following liberalization, beginning with the last decade of the last century, the gap between the rich (mostly urban) and the poor (mostly rural, including a vast majority of the farmers), and thus between the urban and the rural sectors, has increased. The vastly increased consumption in the country has been almost exclusively confined to the middle and the upper classes, living largely in the urban sector. Thus, 78% of our population (which, according to the last census, includes 84% of all dalits, 82% of OBCs, 80% of Muslims, and 85-88% of the unorganised sector including the small and marginal farmers) lives on less than Rs.20 (equivalent to two dollars in terms of price parity) per day. One out of every five Indians is hungry, and 46% of children under three years of age are malnourished according to the latest National Family Health Survey. The dramatic rise of consumerism in India in the present decade has not touched the above 78% of our people.

(e). While the infrastructure in many of the urban areas (e.g. parts of Hyderabad) has undergone an unprecedented and dramatic change (making these areas, perhaps, among the best residential or business districts anywhere), it would be probably impossible to find any rural area in the country where a comparatively similar change has occurred during the last 15 years or so.

(f). Our soil has, in many places, become badly contaminated/eroded, and its productivity substantially decreased on account of excessive use of fertilizers, pesticides and water, even though water is becoming a scarce commodity, with groundwater levels falling drastically year after year in many parts of the country, both rural and urban.

(g). Our overall agricultural productivity has, in most cases, either decreased or increased only marginally.

(h). Our procurement, pricing and public distribution policies, instead of helping people, have created, on the whole, havoc on account of both corruption and intrinsic systemic faults.

(i). Our rural sector comprising over 600,000 villages inhabited mostly by small and marginal farmers is inheritor of a vast repertoire of traditional knowledge and skills (including traditional arts and crafts) which, if commercialized ethically, has the potential of employing at least 100 million people and generating a gross income of over Rs.600,000 crores per year (Annexure 2-A). A vast proportion of this income and employment will be in rural families with a stake in agriculture, thereby empowering the countryside economically and reducing, if not preventing, the drift of population to our bursting cities. It will also help maintain a healthy rate of the agriculture sector's contribution to India's GDP, which has come down from over 40% to below 20%. The effort in the country today to utilize our traditional knowledge and skills for optimal social and economic gain is highly fragmented and largely ineffective, and the condition of a vast majority of those engaged in traditional arts and crafts is pitiful, partly on account of unbridled exploitation by middle-men.

The above list is by no means exhaustive. In spite of a few but notable exceptions to many, if not all, of what has been said above, the present policies, taken all together, cannot be the driver for sustainable food security, farmer security, agriculture security, and the security of our rural sector.

All this calls for drastic changes in our policies concerning agriculture, food production, farmers and the rural sector in general. The increasing population and rising consumption due to rising purchasing power of a few, and the widening gap between the requirement of food and domestic production with the consequent import dependence could seriously affect the country's autonomy in policy-making and imperil internal calm and security by breeding hunger and by aggravating poverty and discontent on a vast scale. And all this could happen earlier than we imagine—say, in a few years.

Our future, therefore, lies in ensuring as soon as possible that our 600,000 villages become places where, on certain counts such as advantage of open space, some people may prefer to live rather than live in cities, as has happened in many other countries. This can only happen when the basic affluence in our villages increases; this can, in turn, happen only when the survival, health and growth of our rural sector (which would include farmers and, therefore, agriculture) is secured on a sustainable basis.

This paper attempts to define the above crisis in detail and suggest means to defuse it.

II. The Immediate Objectives of Agricultural Security

These would be:
(a). Higher productivity, especially of small/marginal farmers, and sufficient production leading to food security.
(b). Larger per capita income in the rural sector that would be in the direction of closing the gap between the rich and the poor in the country.
(c). Substantial increase in employment in the rural sector, with optimum utilisation of knowledge and expertise already existing in the sector.

(d). Connectivity with the urban sector through roads and communication channels.

(e). Education facilities that would enable every child in the rural sector to receive high-quality education up to Class X to begin with and eventually up to Class XII, comparable to that obtained in the urban sector.

(f). Basic, affordable and approachable health facilities with linkages with specialized health and medi-care facilities in the urbanized areas which cannot be replicated in the rural sector.

(g). Environmental security in the rural sector (clean air and water and uncontaminated soil).

(h). Some advantages over those in the urban sector.

III. The Components of Agriculture Security

These are listed in Figure 2.

The problems in regard to most of the items in Figure 2 are mentioned in Section IV, and their possible solutions in Section V.

IV. The Problems

(The Arabic numerals in parenthesis refer to item numbers in Figure 2.)

(i) Seeds (1)

- We often have inadequate availability of certified, quality hybrid seeds that have to be supplied by seed companies (Annexure 2-B).
- Our farmers do not have easy access to checking seed quality.
- Use of hybrids requires farmers to purchase seeds every time. In fact, there will be no seed companies if there were no hybrid

Figure 2

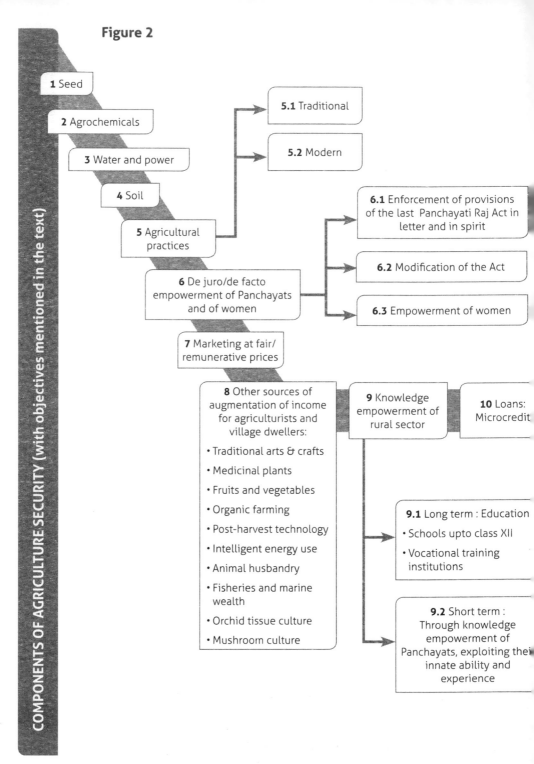

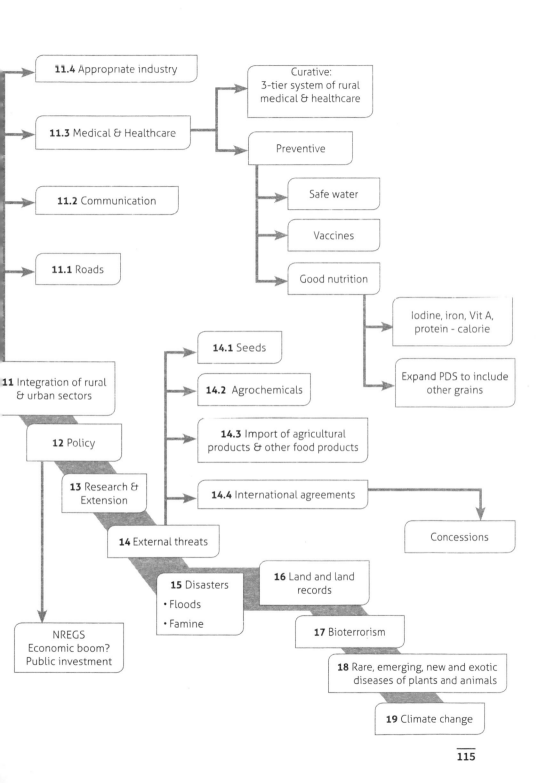

11.4 Appropriate industry

11.3 Medical & Healthcare

Curative:
3-tier system of rural
medical & healthcare

Preventive

Safe water

Vaccines

Good nutrition

Iodine, iron, Vit A,
protein - calorie

Expand PDS to include
other grains

11.2 Communication

11.1 Roads

11 Integration of rural
& urban sectors

12 Policy

13 Research &
Extension

14 External threats

14.1 Seeds

14.2 Agrochemicals

14.3 Import of agricultural
products & other food products

14.4 International agreements

Concessions

15 Disasters
• Floods
• Famine

16 Land and land
records

17 Bioterrorism

18 Rare, emerging, new and exotic
diseases of plants and animals

19 Climate change

NREGS
Economic boom?
Public investment

seeds. Seed companies have vested interest in not propagating true-breeding varieties, of which a large number has been developed by ICAR. The extension capabilities of ICAR must, therefore, be strengthened. The Green Revolution pioneered by the ICAR in the 1960s would not have been possible but for true-breeding varieties.

- There has been an alarming increase in foreign control of seed production which must be curbed (Annexure 2-B).
- While our regulatory systems of plant and animal quarantine have worked well, our regulatory system for permitting release of GM (genetically manipulated) crops grown from GM seeds is highly unsatisfactory (Annexure 2-B).
- We have no effective system of crop insurance to guard against, for example, bad seed or faulty rainfall.

(ii) Agrochemicals and Organic Agriculture (2,8)

We have a strong fertilizer and pesticide lobby which is partially controlled by foreign interests. This lobby not only recommends but ensures through various means (including bribery) excessive use of fertilizers and pesticides, and use of pesticides that should never have been permitted to be used such as chlorpyriphos. We do not make any organised effort to counter this lobby. This inaction has resulted in serious problems in the country. In the case of fertilizers, sometimes as much as 20 times more nitrogen is used compared to what is required to maintain the optimum nitrogen:phosphorous:potassium ratio. This excess nitrogen has extensively contaminated our soil and groundwater. The same is true of pesticides. We have integrated pest management (IPM) available for over 80 crops but we have not used it, even though it has been shown to be extremely effective, and there is a clear statement in the agriculture policy of the Government of India enunciated in 2001 that integrated pest management should be used in the country. In fact, if we had used IPM for cotton for which it was first developed, we would have had no rationale to permit the plantation of Bt cotton in India produced by a foreign company. We also have an enormous repertoire of biopesticides which, again, we do not use: in fact, we do not tell the farmers about it nor give the technology to them. The same would be true of organic agriculture where the future lies. Such agriculture does not use either chemical fertilizers or pesticides. We have all the expertise and resources for organic agriculture. Products of organic agriculture fetch higher prices than products of agriculture using synthetic chemicals. Yet we have not encouraged organic agriculture. The market for products of organic agriculture is growing extremely rapidly—even in India—and if we do not step in, China, which is investing heavily in organic agriculture, will capture it.

At least two efforts (which were fortunately foiled) were made by American organisations (one private and one governmental) in the country to market a spurious agrochemical, or to do research on harmful agrochemicals prohibited elsewhere with a view to market them in India (Bhargava, 2003).

(iii) Water and Power (3)

An easy, short-term and effective solution to substantially augment water supply in the rural sector which has been a major bottleneck in increasing productivity and production in many parts of rural India is rainwater harvesting. Wherever this has been done, for example, substantially in Rajasthan and to a small extent in Andhra Pradesh, the results have been revolutionary. The traditional techniques of rainwater harvesting have been well documented by Narain, Agarwal and Khurana (2001). Yet we have hardly exploited our potential in this area. Therefore, there is a case for taking appropriate steps for rainwater harvesting in the rural sector to augment current programmes of irrigation schemes.

It is now widely recognised that a large number of traditional water storage tanks have silted over the years or dried up, the land being then illegally occupied. Records of location of these tanks are available in the State Archives, for example in the Andhra Pradesh State Archives. They can also be located through remote sensing as has been done in and around Hyderabad. Every effort should be made to resurrect these tanks. This could be the responsibility of national/state water harvesting programmes.

It is ironical that whereas we have shortage of water for agricultural purposes at many places, at many other places, excessive use of (often pumped, underground) water has led to soil damage. This is partly on account of the availability of free power which is neither reliable nor of the right quality. What the farming sector actually needs and desires is not free power but assured and quality power.

(iv) Soil (4)

The country needs a detailed soil map which must be updated periodically and be accessible to every farmer—at least to every village Panchayat. It must record the damage done to the soil in various parts of the country due to excessive use of pesticides and fertilizers and, at times, water. It must also record micronutrient deficiency about which the farmer generally knows very little but the removal of which may be vital for maximizing productivity.

(v) Traditional agricultural practices (5.1)

The Indian Council of Agricultural Research (ICAR) has recently, in five volumes, compiled over 4,000 traditional agricultural practices. This documentation is unparalleled in the history of any country and has been extremely well done. As of December 2005, over 90 of these practices had been validated and close to 40 cross-validated. These should be popularized. Further, there is clearly a need for setting up a system to validate and cross-validate the other documented traditional agricultural practices which could lead to substantial cost reduction and revolutionize our agriculture.

(vi) Modern agricultural practices (5.2)

While our rural sector must be open to modern agricultural practices, their blind acceptance could sow the seeds of disaster. An example would be the use of genetically manipulated (GM) seeds (Annexure 2-B). Before we use them, we must, at the national level, determine if there are other cheaper and conventional alternatives. (This was not done for Bt cotton.) We must then go through an appropriate risk assessment; details of such a risk assessment appropriate for our country are available (Bhargava, 2002). Such a risk assessment for any GM crop will take between 10 and 15 years. If a GM crop goes through successfully such a risk assessment, there is bound to be still some residual risk left which should then be assessed against probable benefits. It is only after all this has been done that a GM crop should be released. As of today, not a single GM crop anywhere in the world has been released following the above risk assessment procedure.

(vii) De juro/de facto empowerment of Panchayats and of women (6)

The 1993 Panchayati Raj Act of the Government of India (which was followed by similar Acts passed by most of the state governments) empowers the Panchayats substantially. However, in practice such empowerment has not always happened. Lok Satta (now an Andhra Pradesh-based political party) had negotiated in 2002-2003 with the Government of Andhra Pradesh for certain powers to be transferred to the Panchayats as per the above Act. Unfortunately, even though there is an official record to say that this should be done, such transfer never took place. A similar exercise must be undertaken by the Centre, and the states persuaded to empower Panchayats appropriately.

The Act as of now vests the financial powers with the Secretary of a Panchayat who is appointed by the government. While the institution of the Panchayat Secretary who provides the link between the lowest and the highest tiers of the government, is appreciated, it is only appropriate that his/her appointment should be made in consultation with the Panchayats, and that the financial powers be exercised jointly by the Secretary and the Panchayats, with the Panchayats having a veto power.

Today, even the most enterprising women in our villages have difficulty in, for example, getting a loan as there is generally no collateral that they can provide. Their professional capability is also curtailed on account of their having to take care of small children during the day.

(viii) Marketing at fair / remunerative price (7)

The minimum support price for an agricultural product must ensure that the primary producer has a reasonable net profit. Further, we must not permit cheap and highly subsidized imports of agricultural products (unprocessed or processed) except to meet real and crucial shortages.

Contract farming should be encouraged but under the condition that the farmers are given a share of the profit that the contracting company makes; one way would be to provide the farmer shares in the company (like ESOPs) under specific but fair conditions. This step, of course, must be in addition to a fair price to the contract farmer. If the farmer believes this price is not fair in relation to the cost of production, s/he should be able to take the case up to a commission empowered or set up to handle such cases (like the Monopolies and Restricted Trade Practices Commission).

The non-functioning of and corruption in Food Corporation of India (FCI) should be a matter of great concern[1].

(ix) Augmentation of income of agriculturists and village dwellers (8)

Some of the ways in which this can be done are listed in Figure 2.

Organic farming has already been mentioned under sub-section (ii) above. A mention has been made of traditional arts and crafts in Section I (i).

Post-harvest technologies can save a large proportion of the (at least) Rs.58,000 crores worth of food that goes to waste in our country every year as stated by the Minister of State for Food Processing in Rajya Sabha[2]. (Estimates of such wastage made by the Ministry of Chemicals and Assochem are 1.5 to more than 2 times higher.)[3]

As regards medicinal plants, we have some 40,000 distinct plant-based drug formulations that have come to us through the four documented traditional systems of medicine (Ayurveda, Unani, Siddha and Tibetian) and the undocumented tribal systems of medicine. We have every reason to believe that at least 4,000 (if not several times more) of these formulations would be validated if tested according to current stringent modes of testing of drugs. If we keep in mind the fact that as of today, on an average, only some 20 new chemical entities (drugs) come into the market every year, and the fact that our country has the capacity to test at least 200 new formulations every year, we can see the potential of India virtually capturing the world's drug market in the next 20 years. The medicinal plants are high-volume products which can complement or substitute traditional agro-products.

As regards fruits and vegetables, India has many uncommon vegetables and fruits and an unparalleled variety of many of them. Thus there are some 150 documented vegetables for which nutritional information is available and perhaps some 50 used by tribals which have not been systematically documented so far. The same is true of fruits. Not only that, the variety we have in each vegetable or fruit is staggering: there are over 400 varieties each of mangoes, okra and brinjal in our National Bureau of Plant Genetic Resources, New Delhi. India has thus the potential of capturing the world's vegetable and fruit market if it could only appropriately publicise its rich heritage in this regard and evolve a marketing strategy involving the hospitality industry (which today serves no more than ten varieties of vegetables or fruits), as happened with bottled water (which was unknown in the US and the UK till the 1960s) at France's initiative. (So, today, hundreds of millions around the world (including in poor India!) drink bottled water even when tap water is perfectly safe or can be made safe by simple procedures such as the use of an appropriate filter.) The price that vegetables and fruits command in terms of produce per acre is much higher than what other food crops bring to the farmer. This would, therefore, be a good way to increase their income, specially of farmers that have small holdings.

A word about orchid tissue culture. The second largest foreign exchange earner for Thailand is believed to be its export of orchids worth apparently Rs.10,000 crores annually. The technique of plant tissue culture was introduced in Thailand only some 30 years ago whereas it has been operative in India for more than 55 years. Not only that, the state of Arunachal Pradesh alone has more than 600 varieties of orchids and its State Forest Research Institute has developed technologies for growing them through tissue culture. Some of them can also be grown in temperate climates in India. In fact, Arunachal Pradesh orchids are recognised as being far more beautiful than the Thai orchids which are much more limited in number, and of which the world now seems to be "tired". Therefore, Arunachal Pradesh has the potential of capturing the world's orchid market and contributing substantially to its own income as well as to the national GDP. Orchids are being grown currently on a small scale in Sikkim, near Darjeeling, and in the Bangalore region, but are not exported.

With our over 8000 km coastline, appropriate temperatures and an extremely rich marine wealth, marine biotechnology has the potential of providing to the world a vast range of products of medicinal and industrial use at a fraction of the cost (in some cases, like poly-unsaturated fatty acids, at a thousand times less cost) at which they are available now. Thus the entire Vitamin A requirement of a child (Vitamin A deficiency being one of the most common and important nutritional deficiencies) in the country can be met at a cost of about Rs.15 per child by natural beta-carotene produced by the marine algae, Donalila.

ICAR has excellent documentation of inefficient energy use in our agriculture.

(x) Knowledge empowerment of the rural sector (9)
All indices of human development relate to knowledge. Therefore, for the rural sector to be a major partner (which it should be in view of its size) in meeting the developmental and societal goals of the country, it must be empowered with knowledge.

The only long-term means of such empowerment is compulsory, free and high-quality education up to Class XII to all children in the age group of 6-18 years, and provision of enough vocational training institutes covering rural and traditional art, craft and skill-specific vocations such as weaving and metal work in our villages.

On a short-term basis, the Panchayats can be provided information packages covering the following items:
  (a). General knowledge that would make them reasonably informed citizens of the country and the world.

(b). Specialised knowledge, e.g. on seeds; optimal use of
fertilizers, water and power; management of live-stock;
output channels; market information; water management
such as rainwater harvesting; technologies for value addition;
time and labour-saving devices; energy plantations, etc. One
would also need to establish a system by which one could
update this knowledge in real time.

(c). Knowledge for immediate use—that is, updated information,
for example, on the weather and the movement of fish, which
one can obtain using satellite imagery.

Items (a) and (b) can be taken care of in 40 hours (one working week)
by carefully selected/trained personnel.

(xi) Loans (10)

The need for a national programme of credit, including micro-credit
for the farming and other self-employed rural communities, is well-
recognised. As of today, less than 3% of the credit available for the
agricultural sector goes to marginal farmers who need it the most.

(xii) Integration of rural and urban sectors (11)

The need for roads to and tele-communication facilities in our villages
is also widely recognised. Fortunately, the government is acutely
aware of this need. The need for giving top priority to this work must
be reiterated continuously.

Industrialisation is, today, a key factor for rapid development, and could
bridge the rural-urban divide, without either sector losing its specific
advantages and character. However, for this to happen, the impetus
for such industrialisation must come from the rural community itself
while the technology and the technical expertise may come from
elsewhere. In fact, our villages have tremendous scope for locating
agriculture-produce-related, environment-friendly industries such

as those using post-harvest and food processing technologies, or producing biofuels, sugar, salt or products of aquaculture (in coastal areas). Special Economic Zones (SEZs) should not be located in existing rural communities. It may be more advantageous to provide concessions to village product-based industries located in or near the villages than to other industries in SEZs.

As regards rural health and medical care, a three-tier system appears to be the most suitable and workable. It would be based on the fact that a vast majority of the population (about 80 per cent?) suffers from less than one per cent of known diseases, most of which can be diagnosed successfully from symptoms and a cure prescribed. A vast proportion of these diseases is caused by contaminated water, lack of sanitation, or lack of adequate nutrition. To diagnose/treat these diseases, one need not be a full-fledged medical doctor or need a laboratory. With an appropriate computer programme such as the one which has been validated by distinguished medical men like Nousher Antia (one of our country's best-known plastic surgeons), an intelligent high-school-pass person can do the job. This person can be provided by the village and helped by the staff that is already attached to primary healthcare centres. What is important is that the appointment of the above-mentioned paramedical staff, which is now made by the central administration of the State, should be made by the local self-government, preferably from local people. It should not be difficult to set up training programmes for such staff. The remaining (perhaps, about 20 per cent) patients should be referred to taluqa/district hospitals which should have all the basic facilities. A system of transporting patients from the village to the taluqa/district hospitals and of the stay of the accompanying persons near the hospital should be an integral part of the programme. A small number of the above 20 per cent of the patients (perhaps, not more than 1-2 per cent of the total patient population) would need to be referred to the closest tertiary care unit in a town/city. The primary and secondary healthcare should be provided by the State, while tertiary care could be provided by private/corporate hospitals (in addition to government hospitals where they exist) and covered by insurance which should be paid for partly by the government and partly by the community concerned.

(xiii) Policy (12)

(a). Continuous review of the National Rural Employment Guarantee Scheme (NREGS) should be made to ensure that (a) payment is adequate, (b) it reaches the intended beneficiaries, and (c) the beneficiary carries out work which is a part of the developmental plan of the region.

(b). It must be recognised that high GDP growth rate does not necessarily benefit rural sector in a commensurate manner. For example, an article by P. Chatterjee (2007) states that child malnutrition and health risk has increased in India (probably more in rural India than in urban India) in spite of the economic boom. Therefore, our liberalization policies must ensure increase in equity concurrently with a high GDP growth rate. Considering that 70% of India is, population-wise, rural and (mostly) agricultural, this means that our liberalization policies must be directed towards making rural India relatively more prosperous, rather than primarily benefiting the well-to-do urban upper and middle class. This would be perhaps the most important step we can take to ensure agricultural security and prevent major internal strife.

(c). There is clearly need for a higher goal and project-directed investment in the agricultural sector.

(xiv) Research (13)

Annexure 2-C lists areas where research needs to be done by the ICAR and the agricultural university system, and where the existing or new information gained through research should be communicated to our agricultural sector.

We have also failed in optimal commercialization of the products of research in the ICAR and agricultural university system. We have not recognised that there are often village or area-specific problems in the rural sector and, therefore, we have not set up a mechanism to handle them.

The value of design, for example in agro implements and in agricultural practice, has not been recognised.

(xv) External threats (14)

(a). The external threats in regard to seeds and agro-chemicals have already been mentioned in sub-sections (i) and (ii) and Annexure 2-B.

(b). In view of the $400 billion annual subsidy to agriculture in the US and Europe which is, in functional terms, orders of magnitude higher than the subsidy we provide to our agriculture, the developed countries are in a position to dump agriculture produce in our country at prices that are lower than our cost of production. Such dumping may have irreversible disastrous effects on our agriculture and must be guarded against. There should, therefore, be a ban on all imports of agriculture produce (unprocessed or processed) except to meet a genuine demand that cannot be locally met. Note must be taken of the recent wheat import which, it appears, did not even satisfy obligatory phytosanitary standards.

(c). We need to carefully review the Indo-US CEO agreement and the Indo-US Knowledge Initiative which have the potential of transferring a substantial part of control of our food business into the hands of foreign organisations.

(xvi) Disasters (15)

The inadequacy of our system to deal with disasters that impact our agriculture is exemplified by (a) the recent Orissa famine when we allowed the import of genetically manipulated soyabean flour from the US, even though we had Food Corporation of India's (FCI) godowns overflowing, and (b) the occurrence of floods (with floods and famine occurring in the same area at different times of the year). There is, therefore, a need for setting up an Agriculture Disaster Rapid Action Force and an effective flood control system for working out means to prevent floods (for example by diverting and then collecting flood waters), for which precedents exist in the country.

(xvii) Land Records (16)

Land records are not complete and not maintained in most parts of the country. Further, whereas we need to bring more land under cultivation, the SEZs are alienating valuable agricultural lands.

(xviii) Bioterrorism (17)

We have not adequately recognised the possibility and consequences of biological warfare against, or a terrorist attack using biological weapons on, our agricultural crops or our animal wealth.

(xix) Rare, emerging, new and exotic diseases of plants and animals (18)

One of the outstanding successes (unfortunately not widely known) of the ICAR has been the prevention of entry of new and rare diseases of animals that have not existed in the country by the High Security Animal Lab of the ICAR at Bhopal which, in spite of its outstanding facilities [it being the only lab in India with the highest (P4) level of containment facility] and performance, is just a unit of the Indian Veterinary Research Institute at Izatnagar. No such facility exists in the country for identification and handling of rare, emerging, new and exotic diseases of plants.

(xx) Effect of climate change

There is new awareness that climate change can progressively affect agricultural output, such as of wheat; this should be factored in our future objectives.

V. Recommendations

(The Arabic numerals in parenthesis at the end of a para refer to item numbers in Figure 2. A few other related recommendations are mentioned in the text.)

A. The recommendations made in the report of the last National Farmers Commission that was submitted to the Government of India by its Chairman, Dr M S Swaminathan, which also speaks about agricultural security and emphasizes (among other measures) the need for appropriate credit facilities for farmers, should be accepted in principle and appropriate action taken on it expeditiously.

B. A system needs to be set up to ensure adequate availability of seeds by, perhaps, revamping Seed Corporation of India. Seed production must be in our own hands, with no Foreign Direct Investment (FDI) normally permitted in this sector. In special cases where there is a clear, transparently established benefit to India which cannot be accrued in any other way, up to 25 per cent FDI may be permitted in the seed sector. An appropriate seed bill needs to be passed to ensure this. Seed subsidies (a source of corruption today) should be replaced by provision of quality seeds at the market price. (1, 14.1)

C. A set of seed-testing laboratories which can be easily accessed by farmers through seed collection centres should be set up in the public sector. They should be capable of testing GM seeds and establishing seed identity through DNA fingerprinting. (The research component of DNA fingerprinting of seeds is being already taken care of by an ICAR set-up in Delhi.) An effective, fair, socially relevant, scientifically sound, transparent and professionally managed regulatory and supervisory system should be set up for evaluation and release of genetically modified organisms (GMOs). (The present system does not satisfy these criteria.) (1)

D. An appropriate system of crop insurance should be set up, for example as a safeguard against supply of bad seed. If the seed is supplied by a seed company, the company should pay a part of the premium, such a scheme replacing the system of penalties for supply of bad seed.

E. Integrated Pest Management (IPM) technologies and biopesticides developed by ICAR must be used as a matter of policy, in preference to synthetic pesticides or the so-called pest-resistant GM crops. Standard Operative Procedures should be prepared for Integrated Pest Management (which would drastically reduce the use of synthetic pesticides and thus contamination of soil and groundwater) for various crops, in all Schedule VIII languages. An industrial set-up should be put in place, through an initiative of the ICAR, to produce various requirements for IPM. The ICAR should set up a National Quality Control Laboratory for material used in IPM. A strategy for dissemination of procedures of IPM should be worked out. An appropriate number of ITIs should be set up for training in IPM at various levels, some within the ICAR system itself. (2)

F. The existing subsidy on fertilizers should be reduced or eliminated depending on the size of the agricultural land holding. A Soil Atlas for the country should be prepared (if one is not already available), kept updated and made available widely to farmers. (2, 4, 14.2)

G. An empowered Rainwater Harvesting Authority should be set up in every state as well as at the Centre. The Central authority should document and disseminate the success stories in this regard, for example, in Rajasthan, West Bengal and Gujarat. The policy of free power should be replaced by a policy of providing quality and assured power at cost. The financial implications of resorting to drip irrigation (to save water and prevent overuse of water) should be investigated on the national scale, and the technique resorted to wherever possible and economically feasible. The government needs to evolve a rational policy for water use and groundwater extraction, treating water as a commodity, which could be charged. (3)

H. A national mission should be set up for validation of our over 4,000 traditional agricultural practices and commercialization of the validated ones. The mission should involve the National Innovation Foundation and the Indian Council of Agricultural Research; it could become a model of cooperation between government and civil society in an area which is of the utmost importance to the country. (5.1)

I. The ICAR should set up a permanent panel for assessment of new technologies from outside India; the panel should consist of people with high public credibility and established competence, integrity, courage, and commitment to our agriculture and the country; it should include scientists, economists, sociologists and farmers. (5.2)

J. A rational policy for farm labour must be evolved. A knowledge-based policy for use of agricultural land should be framed. Farmers with small holdings should be encouraged to produce high value crops. (5)

K. Elections to the two lowest levels of local self-government (the Panchayats and the Panchayat Samithis) should be depoliticized de facto, as per constitutional requirements, by the Election Commission. All possible steps must be taken for true empowerment of Panchayats in accordance with the provisions of the 1993 Panchayati Raj Act. Panchayats should have a say in the selection of Secretaries to the Panchayats. There should be greater devolution of financial powers to Panchayats. Adult education should concentrate on rural women who should have a legal right over agricultural lands belonging to their respective husbands. The government, including village administration, should provide crèches in villages to enable women to be mobile. (6.1, 6.2, 6.3)

L. The minimum procurement price and the minimum selling price of a primary agro-product should ensure a fair return to the farmers; they should be determined with the active involvement of the farmer community, and should ideally be, specially in the latter case, the market price. The FCI should be wound up and replaced by creation of local storage facilities and local buffer staff, procured and managed by the local self government such as the Panchayat. Contract farming should be encouraged under conditions specified in Section III (viii). Marginal and small farmers (with less than 4 acres of land holding) should be encouraged to grow high-value crops such as medicinal plants, vegetables and fruits, and an appropriate system of collection, processing and marketing of their produce (a system in which the farmers have a stake/share) involving the private sector should be evolved. It should be recognised that traceability of a farm product, or its having been grown organically (item N below), fetches significantly higher prices for the crop. An appropriate task force should be set up for popularizing our enormous repertoire of traditional fruits and vegetables; this should be done in collaboration with the private sector (for example, our leading hotels) and the ICAR. No import of any agriculture produce (unprocessed or processed) should be permitted excepting to meet a genuine demand that cannot be met from sources within the country. The role of traders in agro-products must be regulated to ensure that the maximum benefit comes to primary producers and processors. (7, 8, 14.3)

M. A national mission should be set up for ethical commercialization of our traditional creative, cultural and legacy industries, which will also bring work in these areas, currently under various ministries (some 10 of them), under one umbrella. (8)

N. A set of new institutional mechanisms (perhaps corporations or cooperatives) should be set up to encourage organic farming (that is, organic agriculture). The ICAR should set up a separate institute as a national centre for research and development in organic agriculture. Alternatively, the ICAR could convert one of its existing institutes to an institute devoted to organic agriculture. The government should set up a group to define standards for products of organic agriculture for domestic market labelling. (8)

O. The government should set up a Mission on post-harvest technologies to, among others, collect, collate, document and transmit relevant information to stakeholders; set phytosanitary standards; ensure traceability of products; set up appropriate training programmes; devise marketing strategies; identify investors; and ensure that the first step in post-harvest processing is taken by the primary producer and that he continues to be a stakeholder in all subsequent steps including marketing. This Mission should also engage large business houses to invest in post-harvest processing, rather than in retail of primary agricultural produce which is currently destroying the livelihood of many. (8)

P.	The nine new energy-saving technologies developed by the ICAR so far should be promoted through an appropriate mechanism. The National Energy Policy should include energy generation from surplus biomass and crop residue, for the exploitation of which an appropriate consortium should be set up. The importance of continued use of biomass, such as firewood, in the rural sector must be recognised, and mechanisms for increasing the efficiency and convenience of such use (such as smokeless *chulahs*), and propagating them should be worked out. A well thought-out programme of energy plantations (social forestry) should be implemented. A revolving fund for entrepreneurs (with a corpus of say Rs.1,000 crores) should be set up for community biogas plants. (8)

Q.	Animal husbandry, fisheries, agriculture, fertilizers and other agro-chemicals should be brought under a single department of the government. (8)

R.	Steps must be taken to establish culture of mushrooms or orchid tissue culture industry (for both of which technologies are available in the country) to supplement farmers' income in states such as Arunachal Pradesh. Special incentives should be provided to those setting up a marine biotechnology industry. Rural produce-based industries must be set up in the rural sector in a way that the primary producer has a stake in them, as also mentioned in item (O). (8, 11.4)

S.	It should be ensured over a specified period (of say, 10 years) that every village child between the age of 6 and 18 is enrolled in a high-quality school of the standard of a good Central School. Education in such schools must be free and compulsory, and must include trade-training involving use of one's own hands (e.g. in agriculture in schools located in the rural sector), specially in the last 4-6 years of higher secondary school (10+2). (To make this possible for the whole country, it is estimated that 400,000 Central School-type schools would be needed, some 70 per cent of which will need to be located in our villages.) The number of vocational training institutions should be increased ten-fold (from about 5,000 to 50,000) with most of the new ones being located in rural areas. The number of vocations covered by such institutions should be increased several-fold, and include those of relevance to rural communities, such as organic agriculture, use of fertilizers, preparation of organic manure, pest-control, weaving, and metal work. An appropriate system of empowering farmers through knowledge that would make them less prone to exploitation and more productive, on a continuing basis, must be evolved. This could include preparation and dissemination of information packages for Panchayats as mentioned in Section III (x), setting up of village libraries in schools, establishing Village Resource Centres as envisaged by the M S Swaminathan Research Foundation, and setting up 50,000 Knowledge Clubs, each club taking care of a village cluster and having a budget of Rs.1 lakh per year. (9.1, 9.2)

T. An effective national programme of credit, including micro-credit, for the marginal and small farmers and other self-employed rural communities, should be instituted. It should be ensured that loans earmarked for the agriculture sector go primarily to marginal and small farmers. Self-help groups should be multiplied and supported, e.g. through microcredit. Priorities must be accorded to establishing connectivity of the rural sector with the urban sector through roads and telecommunication which would, for example, include tele-medicine. A three-tier rural medical and healthcare system along the lines mentioned in Section III (xii) should be set up, perhaps first on an experimental basis as a part of the existing rural health mission and medicare programme. The existing mission to provide potable water to every resident of every village must be given top priority and made time-bound. To provide better nutrition, the production of pulses should be substantially augmented. The Public Distribution System (PDS) should include them as well as grains other than those already included. It should be decentralized and brought under the local self-government to make it fair and efficient, which it is not today. Steps (such as those mentioned earlier) should be taken to make the NREGS maximally effective and productive. All possible steps should also be taken to increase (double) the contribution of agriculture to GDP so that GDP growth decreases inequities. Goal-directed project-based funding to rural sector must be increased substantially. The funds released by withdrawal of fertilizer, power and seed subsidies, could be used to finance some of the other support systems for the rural sector recommended in this paper. (10, 11.1, 11.2, 11.3, 12)

U. The ICAR should consider investing in research and extension work in selected areas listed in Annexure 2-C. Further, a suitable mechanism such as an effective Agriculture Research Development Corporation (on the lines of the National Research Development Corporation) should be set up to commercialise the results of agricultural research in the country. The value of setting up a National Institute of Agricultural Design, with the help of National Institute of Design, Ahmedabad, should be examined. There is a need for revamping and restructuring (total reorganisation, both qualitatively and quantitatively) of our rural extension programmes, keeping in mind that inappropriately done extension work can cause more harm than good. In the absence of any good governmental extension programme, this job is being done by multinational corporations (MNCs) to the great detriment of our agriculture security. It was the high quality and the massive extent of extension work done by ICAR that brought the first Green Revolution. ICAR today needs some 5000 additional extension workers to optimally utilize its capabilities and output. The ICAR must extend its Krishi Vigyan

Kendras (KVKs) programme to cover every district. The KVKs must not only be involved in proactively empowering the farmers with relevant knowledge and engage in extension work, but must also identify and help solve district/region-specific agriculture-related problems. The budget of ICAR should be increased sufficiently to enable it to implement the above recommendations. (13)

V. It must be ensured that our foreign agreements that relate to agriculture, like the ones mentioned earlier, are reviewed periodically and used transparently in our national interest. (14.4)

W. An Agriculture Disaster Rapid Action Force should be set up. An effective flood control system should also be set up, learning lessons from successes in parts of the country such as the North-East. (15)

X. Land records must be fully straightened out and updated electronically in the entire country as has been done or is being done in some states such as West Bengal, Kerala and Andhra Pradesh. No agricultural land should be alienated to SEZs. On the contrary, a crash programme of bringing additional land (say, 5-10 million hectares per year) under cultivation should be started. This land could be given to marginal farmers (with a land holding of less than 2 hectares), around which new modern villages could come up. (16)

Y. A strategy should be worked out to make our agricultural scientists, managers and policymakers become aware, on a continuing basis, of the use of, identification of, and protection from agents of biological warfare against our agricultural crops, farm animals and poultry. The High Security Animal Lab of ICAR in Bhopal should be converted into a National Centre for Animal Disease Control, and a new Centre for Plant Disease Control should be set up to prevent the entry of in the country, identify, and work out measures to combat, rare, exotic and emerging diseases affecting animals or plants, respectively. Our rules for importing plants (including seeds) and animals should be revisited, made appropriately stringent where they are not so, and implemented strictly. (17, 18)

Z. To address all the above, a high-power suitably empowered apex body chaired by the Agriculture Minister should be set up to examine in detail the above recommendations and work out mechanisms to implement those that are found to be worthy of implementation. One of the functions of the proposed apex body should be to put together every year reliable data on production (and productivity, for example per person, per animal, per unit land, or per rupee spent, as appropriate) as well as consumption per person of foodgrains, pulses, fruits, vegetables, milk, poultry, marine food, and meat. This data should be presented to the government and the public along with the data for the preceding nine years and the population data. As a matter of policy, any obligatory import of food items recommended by the apex body should be "compensated" for by at least an equivalent export of primary or value-added agro-product. Estimates should also be provided of food material wasted due to insects and pests, or on account of lack of storage, transport and processing facilities. The proposed apex body must take an integrated view of food security, farmer security, agriculture security and security of our rural sector, and take steps to ensure all of them. One of its major objectives should be to optimally utilize our national potential in the agriculture/rural sector and in the related traditional knowledge sector which is largely village-based. It should, for example, determine the best manner in which the resources released by abolition of various subsidies (e.g. on power, seeds and fertilizers) and of FCI, and reorganisation of PDS, can be used to meet the above objective. If all that is recommended here is done, our rural sector could account for more than 40 per cent of GDP in the next 10 to 12 years.

Employment and Wealth Generation Potential of Traditional Knowledge (TK)

(i) EMPLOYMENT POTENTIAL (Based on the 2001 census)

		(number, in crores)
1.	**Non-workers**	
	Total 62.64 crores	
	44% (27.56 crores) can work	
	40% of 27.56 crores can work in TK sector	11.02
2.	**Agricultural workers: cultivators**	
	(10.20 crores) *	
	20% of them can work in TK sector	2.04
3.	**Agricultural workers: labour**	
	(12.06 crores) *	
	One-sixth of them can work in TK sector	2.01
4.	**Other workers: rural sector**	
	(10.48 crores)	
	50% of them can work in TK sector	5.24
5.	**Other workers: urban sector**	
	(4.72 crores)	
	25% of them can work in TK sector	1.18
		21.49
		(215 million)
	Very conservative figure:	100 million

*approximate

(ii) INCOME GENERATION POTENTIAL PER YEAR

(Rs.in crores) *

Plant–based drugs (10 x 10,000 crores) (international annual market for one drug for Hepatitis B from *Phyllanthus amarus* estimated at $6-18 billion, say $10 b = 45,000 crores)	100,000
Rainwater harvesting (100 x 100 crores) (value Rs.100 per person on an average, per year, excluding water for agriculture) (0.3 paise / litre, based on 100 litre / person / day)	10,000
Preventable loss of agricultural produce due to pests using traditional methods (25% lost; 75% preventable)	100,000
Marketing of new (traditionally used) vegetables and fruits plus value addition by food processing (target 1 billion population @ Euros 30 each / year)	150,000
20% value addition to 33% of our existing agriculture produce through organic farming	35,000
New areas for tourism where Traditional Knowledge, Traditional Practices, or Cultural and Creative Work is exhibited (10 million tourists spending on an average 100 Euros extra)	5,000
Creative and cultural industries	200,000

Total   **Rs.600,000**

Note: Present value of marketed agricultural produce (approx. 20% of GDP of $600 billion or Rs.27,00,000 crores): Rs.540,000 crores.

*approximate, rounded off values

On Foreign Control of Seed Production

(1) Role of seeds in the power-game

The food industry, based primarily on agriculture, is the largest industry in the world. Mankind can survive without arms, medicines or even housing (as it has done in the past) but cannot survive without food. Food security was the only security that primitive man worked towards; it is food security that made the human species survive on our planet. Therefore, those who control food production around the world would control the world. To control food production, one needs to control only seed production and agro-chemicals production. Table 1 gives some details of the major seed producers in the world. The effort of such foreign interests towards acquiring *total* control of our seed business is, therefore, something we must guard against.

(2) How do they do it?

(i)   Traditionally, farmers had total control over their seeds. They could keep them, barter them, sell them, or sow them themselves. Our recent Plant Varieties and Farmers' Rights Protection Act notified in 2005 allows the farmers to do exactly this. As long as farmers did so, there were no seed companies. They came into existence because of development of hybrid seeds, the progeny of which cannot be reused (if reused, they will not give the same results as the original hybrids). Development of new hybrid seeds by seed companies is, therefore, one important way of acquiring control over seed production. If these companies are foreign companies or Indian companies controlled financially by foreign interests, and if their market share and our dependence on them progressively increases, we would also progressively lose agricultural security. As of today, their market share could be about 30% which must ring an alarm bell.

(ii) The seed companies develop new technologies such as genetically modified seeds, and then they sell these technologies—as they have done in India—by persuading and influencing governments at various levels. They resort to bribery (as Monsanto did in Indonesia for Bt cotton seeds). They prevent indigenous development and break all laws of the land, as has happened in respect with Bt cotton in India. (For details, see Bhargava, 2003.)

(iii) In the absence of an appropriate and effective regulatory and supervisory system in the country, seed companies have resorted to illegal plantation of unapproved crops, such as genetically manipulated (GM) crops. There are many documented instances of such crops being planted in India (e.g. Navbharat's Bt cotton in Gujarat) which, in some cases, were uprooted by vigilant non-governmental organisations.

(iv) Another way is to contaminate the food chain in the country through illegal genetically manipulated food material. Since most of Europe and Japan have stringent laws about import and marketing of GM food, more than the prescribed percentage of GM food in the food product would prevent its export to Europe and Japan. A very well-known and highly-publicized case was that of Zambia. When the country went through one of its worst famines recently, a developed country offered it GM corn. However, Zambia's government refused this corn and said they would appreciate if instead of corn, corn flour was sent. Their fear was that once the GM corn comes in, some farmers would be tempted to sow it and this could contaminate their own crops and other agricultural crops as well, the produce of which was being exported to Europe. This will have a serious repercussion on their exports. However, the donor country refused to donate corn flour instead of corn seed.

(v)   In fact, selling or taking any GM crop to any country is illegal under the Cartagena protocol, unless the recipient country is informed and has accepted receipt of such GM food or crop; yet this practice has been widely resorted to. For example, when we had famine in Orissa and our government did not release grain in spite of the FCI godowns overflowing with 60 million tonnes of food grain, the US sent us soyabean flour which was eventually established to be flour prepared from GM soyabean and which could not be marketed in the host country. This was done without Indian government's approval.

(vi)   There is evidence that foreign companies that operate, for example, in the area of seeds, fudge their data and propagate untruths about the results of their products. For example, what has been said about the success of Bt cotton is far from what the ground reality appears to be according to careful studies done by responsible NGOs as well as the Government. In fact, there is strong documentary evidence that the 1044 suicides of farmers in Vidarbha as of January last were related to the failure of Bt cotton.

(vii)   Foreign organisations concerned with agriculture also influence the governmental machinery in other ways. For example, when Monsanto's Bt cotton failed in parts of Andhra Pradesh, and the government finally accepted this failure, they asked the company to pay compensation to the farmers as per the rules. There is incontrovertible evidence available, which establishes that the data was fudged so that the compensation that the company had to pay to the farmers was much less than what they should have paid. Even this compensation has still not been paid.

(viii)   The foreign interests that have entered into India in the seed business have used false publicity to establish the superiority of their seeds, such as of Bt cotton. On this basis, they price their seeds very high. In the case of Bt cotton, the pricing by Monsanto was close to four times that of non-Bt seeds. The difference was supposed to be the trait value. Again, after much vacillation and under pressure from farmers and responsible NGOs, the Government took the case to the Monopolies and Restricted Trade Practices Commission which gave a verdict against the company; the company has agreed to cut its price by a factor of nearly two but it is still much higher than what it should be.

TABLE 1 of Annexure 2-A

World's Top 11 Seed Companies

S.No.	Company	2004 Seed Sales (millions of US dollars)
1	Monsanto (US) + Seminis (acquired by Monsanto)	$2,277 + $526 = $2,803
2	Dupont / Pioneer (US)	$2,600
3	Syngenta (Switzerland)	$1,239
4	Groupe Limagrain (France)	$1,044
5	KWS AG (Germany)	$622
6	Land O' Lakes (US)	$538
7	Sakata (Japan)	$416
8	Bayer Crop Science (Germany)	$387
9	Taikii (Japan)	$366
10	DLF-Trifolium (Denmark)	$320
11	Delta & Pine Land (US)	$315

Source: ETC Group Global Seed Industry Concentration Report 2005

Areas of Research/Extension Work to Meet Needs of Farmers

The following topics (randomly arranged) that relate to the felt needs of farmers are suggested for further research by ICAR and other organisations:

*(1) Post-harvest technology including technologies for value addition, such as food processing.

(2) Water harvesting using traditional technologies.

(3) New agriculture product storage technologies, particularly for decentralized storage.

(4) Veterinary genetics and pathology (including microbiology and virology), for example, sequencing of genomes of animals specially widely used in India, such as buffaloes; and developing genetically engineered vaccines for diseases such as FMV and rinderpest.

*(5) Organic agriculture and associated activities such as vermiculture.

(6) Developing methodologies for quick marker-aided selection.

*(7) Integrated pest management: to increase experience and range of applications and modifications where necessary.

(8) Introduction of hybrid vigour into pure-breeding varieties.

(9) Setting up of commercial DNA fingerprinting of plants and seeds. Also documentation to help farmers ensure that they do not get spurious seeds.

(10) Development of osmo-resistant varieties (collaboration with MSSRF at Chennai, and CCMB at Hyderabad), and encouragement of commercial plant tissue culture for producing products such as vanillin.

(11) Better weather prediction models (in collaboration with DST and MST Radar Facility of the Department of Space at Tirupati).

(12) Identification of varieties of medicinal plants that would have high amounts of markers correlated with activity.

(13) Development of technologies for use of agricultural waste products.

(14) Technologies that could increase productivity and release time, labour and resources of farmers which could be utilized for additional employment.

(15) Identification of avenues for additional employment and research on making them attractive and lucrative enough for farmers to engage in them.

*(16) A socio-economic analysis of the use of energy in agriculture, along with energy saving mechanisms and strategies for energy management.

(17) Development and propagation of technologies for controlled release of fertilizers and pesticides.

(18) Systems approach towards commercialisation of existing technologies such as for orchid tissue culture in Arunachal Pradesh.

(19) Metabolic engineering to generate more value (e.g. transferring genes of maize for enzymes such as phosphoenol pyruvate carboxylasc/oxygenase and orthophosphate dikinase into rice for increasing yield).

(20) An in-depth study of 'shifting agricultural practices', for example, in Arunachal Pradesh, to increase its efficiency.

These areas should be pursued by carefully selected, competent and committed scientists in a mission mode, with clear time-targets, appropriate funding based on milestones, freedom from bureaucratic hassles but professional, social and financial accountability. ICAR has already organised meetings in the areas marked with an asterisk (*), during 2005-2006, that have come up with specific recommendations, the more important of which are included in Section V.

Notes

1. Dilip Cherian, Questions galore about future of FCI, *Deccan Chronicle*, Hyderabad, 10th June 2007, p.7.
2. News report, *The Times of India*, Hyderabad, 12th May 2002.
3. News report, *The Economic Times*, Delhi, 9th June 2006.

References

Bhargava, P M, "High Stakes in Agro Research: Resisting the Push", *Economic and Political Weekly*, 23rd August 2003, pp. 3537–3542.

Bhargava, P M, "GMOs: Need for Appropriate Risk Assessment System", *Economic and Political Weekly*, 13th April 2002, pp. 1402–1406.

Narain, S, Agarwal, A, and Khurana, I, "Making Water Everybody's Business", Centre for Science and Environment, New Delhi, 2001.

Chatterjee, P, *The Lancet*, Vol. 369, 2007, p. 1417.

IV
EPILOGUE

The conclusion is that in nine years, beginning 2004, the performance of UPA Government has been dismal. This has been unfortunate, as we had many expectations from Mrs Sonia Gandhi and Dr Manmohan Singh given the qualities they have, and the unprecedented opportunities that the UPA Government has had.

Understanding the why and how of such a dismal performance would require an extensive, professional socio-politico-economic analysis which we are not capable of engaging in. All that we have done is to look at it all from the perspective of responsible and concerned citizens.

We are not connected with any political party. Unfortunately, none of them offers us much hope. Yet we are optimistic for we trust our civil society if not our "uncivil" governments.

V

MOVING FORWARD

FURTHER STEPS NEEDED AS OF MAY 2013, IN ADDITION TO THOSE
STATED IN PART II, TO SOLVE SOME OF OUR MAJOR PROBLEMS

The Agenda for the Nation was prepared in 2003—that is, some ten years ago. If one wants to plan for the future, one would need to take into account what has happened in these ten years. In the following pages, and the 11 Appendices of this part, we state in some detail what needs to be done, in addition to what has been listed earlier, by a responsible and responsive government in Delhi, supported appropriately by the state governments. In fact, action should have been taken on all these points by now by the governments but nothing substantial seems to have been done so far in regard to almost all the action points listed in this part of this book.

The authors seek the indulgence of the reader for any repetition they may consider unnecessary. What follows is, in a way, an addendum to the expectations that we listed in the Agenda in 2003 (Part II of this book). Most of the material in this part of the book has been discussed with and presented in writing to the Prime Minister at his request, on 14th and 15th July, and 5th November, 2012, at his office and residence on 7, Race Course Road, New Delhi. Even though the Prime Minister was extremely receptive to what is stated in the following pages, unfortunately, as of writing this part (May 2013), very little action has been taken to take care of the expectations listed on the following pages, or the expectations listed in Part II which have not been so far met.

(1) Education:
- The Right to Education Act passed and notified in 2010 was considered by us as unimplementable and, as expected, has not been implemented anywhere (as an example, see Appendices 1 and 2). We must work towards progressive de-commercialisation of school education and setting up a Common School System. Such a strategy will also lead to progressive "dereservation" over a 10-12 year period.

- The Yashpal Committee Report (of which the summary of recommendations is reproduced in Appendix 3) must be implemented in toto to take care of the problems plaguing our higher education system, such as commercialisation and lack of quality and quantity. [Over 80 per cent of the products of today's highly expensive higher education system (including engineers and doctors) are unemployable. None of our universities, including IITs and IISc, are in the top 200 worldwide.]
- In regard to our universities collaborating with foreign universities, the recent recommendations of the UGC (summarized in Appendix 4) must be made mandatory.
- The allocation of funds and the quantum of release should be the same as the Plan outlay on education. There was a wide gap between these in the 11th Plan, for example in respect of UGC. Further, the total allocation should be increased to 6 per cent in a time-bound manner.
- UGC, for nearly two years, till February 2011, had only an Acting Chairman. The events that led to this situation were shameful, must be analysed, and lessons learnt so that they are not repeated in the future.
- A new road map must be drawn for our vocational education system which would take into account our traditional arts and crafts that can generate very substantial employment and revenues. We need some 2,00,000 vocational training institutions that would substantially increase the scope of our vocational training and would train those who have studied only up to, say, Class VI on the one hand as well as those who have a degree on the other. Today's 5000 or so vocational training institutes in our country are very limited in their scope and inaccessible to a vast majority of those who would benefit from such training and, in turn, provide the much needed benefit to the society which today badly lacks even plumbers, carpenters and masons.

(2) Health:

- Please see the article (Appendix 5) by one of us on the edit page of *The Hindu* of 14th July, 2012, for a statement of problems plaguing our medical and healthcare (medicare) system. For example, we have the world's worst mortality rate for children below 5 years, over 26 million such children dying in 2011. The following steps, in addition to those implied in the above article, will help take care of our major medicare problems.

- We should aim towards following the British pattern of National Health Service, that is General Practitioner (GP) or Family Physician–based, to begin with in the urban areas. No specialist should see a patient unless the patient has been first seen by a GP.

- Recognising that our villages today are often devoid of many basic facilities and would not be able to retain a person with an MBBS degree coming from outside, we would need to adopt a second-best implementable strategy to take care of rural medicare, keeping in mind that in the rural areas a large proportion of health problems are a consequence of lack of availability of potable water. Further, both in rural and urban areas, a vast proportion (over 90%!) of the sick and the unwell suffer from a very small number of common disorders where one can go directly from symptom to cure. This situation can be exploited to train a bright young high-school pass person to use an appropriate computer programme (prototype of which is available and had been tested by the late Dr N Antia) to take care of some 80% of medical and health problems in the rural sector. The programme will identify the 20% or so that would need more advanced medicare including the use of diagnostic tests. Arrangements should be made by Panchayats through appropriate budgetary provision to transport the above 20% patients to the nearest government hospital equipped with all secondary care facilities including accommodation for accompanying members of family (one room with two beds and meals for two persons to be provided free). The above facilities at the village level could be built around an appropriately located primary health centre with appropriate number of trained health workers like ASHA (at least one male and one female for each village or cluster of adjacent villages as appropriate). The basic requirements (such as medicines) of a primary village health centre must be defined and provided in real time on a continuing basis. The staff at the above centres must be well integrated within the village community, and be available for help at their residence if required, and should be, as far as possible, derived from the villages it serves.

- The government hospitals providing secondary and tertiary medical care must be appropriately upgraded and maintained so that they can regain the trust of the people they had enjoyed till large-scale commercialization of healthcare began. Every patient who comes there must be first seen by a GP, unless referred to a specialist by a GP.

- In addition, where possible (e.g. in some rural areas and all urban areas), Family Physicians (with at least an MBBS degree but preferably an MD in family medicine) must be appointed (and given proper facilities, both personal and professional) to take care of specified areas.

- All private medical colleges—except those run by Trusts in letter and law—should be, over an appropriate period of time, taken over by the government after appropriate preparation and, as far as possible, transferred to a nearby state-run university. Entrance into them should be through a national examination and means independent (details can be provided). They should be governed by the provisions of the Yashpal Committee Report.

- All private hospitals including corporate hospitals should be converted into charitable trusts or Section 25 companies. They could be categorised into groups (say, I to V) depending on their quality and facilities. Each hospital would have a general ward and rooms categorised into three or four categories. All treatments in the hospital plus stay in the general ward would be reimbursed by the government, irrespective of the category of the hospital. The rest of the room expenses will be borne by the sponsoring organisation (which could be a government organisation itself) or by the patient. What is important is that these hospitals will only admit patients referred to by a government GP or a government hospital—and will provide only specialised tertiary care. There would be one member of the government and one nominee of civil society chosen by the government on the Board of Trustees or the Board of Directors of the hospital. If need be, they would be provided a block grant by the government.

- All hospitals and diagnostic centres must be required to be accredited by NABH and NABL, respectively.
- A system of accreditation of infertility clinics should be set up.
- The government must have the option of taking over corporate or other private hospitals with appropriate compensation.
- 'Arogyashree' programmes must be discontinued in a phased manner and replaced by free service in upgraded, efficiently run and adequately financed government hospitals.
- Government must not support or encourage unscientific healthcare practices such as homeopathy.
- Only those who have been appropriately trained may prescribe allopathic drugs. Thus village health workers mentioned above will be authorized to prescribe/give only those drugs that the computer programme tells them to do. Anyone formally trained in any other system of medicine or practising it must not be allowed to prescribe any allopathic drug which is not an OTC drug—even if the person is given a short-term training in modern pharmacology (as the Maharashtra Government intends to do).
- All government doctors and all hospitals must prescribe and use generics instead of branded drugs.

- Severe action must be taken against those producing sub-standard or fake drugs. For this purpose, an effective national testing facility should be set up.
- An ethical code of conduct for medical practitioners and medical education should be prepared and implemented; cases where it is breached must be publicized widely (for a glimpse of widely used unethical medical and healthcare practices, see Appendix 5).
- A system must be set up to ensure the content-wise authenticity and safety of imported foreign-branded foodstuff made in India, for example for its content of toxic or GM material. An example would be a foreign brand of stackable potato chips which is alleged to contain little potato but a fair amount of acrylamide—a potent carcinogen.

(3) Water:
- Rainwater harvesting must be vigorously pursued, both in the rural and the urban sectors, with appropriate financial support in the rural sector and legal compulsion in the urban sector (for details of implementable-traditional methodologies, see *Making Water Everybody's Business; Practice and policy of water harvesting*, by Anil Agarwal, Sunita Narain and Indira Khurana, published by Centre for Science and Environment, New Delhi).
- Traditional tanks (e.g. those identified by NRSA) must be resuscitated wherever possible and no further loss of such tanks to human greed should be allowed.
- Sources of potable water (existing or potential) must be identified/ created in every village. In the case of potential sources, methodology for making it potable must be communicated to the Panchayats and implementation ensured.
- Flood waters from rivers should be diverted into canals/reservoirs (new where possible) for use during the rest of the year.

(4) Energy:

* All existing sources of renewable energy (e.g. biomass, wind, mini- and micro-hydel) should be fully exploited with emphasis on local generation.
* A substantial investment must be made (through a separate institution) on research in and application of solar power, using all available technologies and methodologies, drawing lessons from countries such as Germany.
* Similarly, we must invest on a priority basis in alcohol production from grass.
* Energy plantations for which detailed plans were made when DNES (now MHES) was set up should be encouraged in the rural sector where firewood is and can continue to be used.
* There must be a relook at our emphasis on nuclear energy.
* Possible use of new technologies, such as induced hydraulic fracturing, must be investigated.

(5) Corruption:

* We should learn a lesson from the events in Andhra Pradesh, since 2004, and refrain from promoting people who are known to be corrupt and law-breakers.
* Corruption charges against or impeachment of a judge must not be dropped if s/he resigns.
* Agencies investigating corruption must be made autonomous constitutionally.
* An appropriate Lokpal Bill acceptable to civil society must be passed as early as possible.
* No case of corruption should be shielded by the State. In fact, speedy action to settle the cases against allegedly corrupt people, irrespective of their position, would be an important step in the direction of containing corruption.

- Concerted and serious effort should be made to unearth black money and declare it as a national asset.

(6) Science & Technology (S&T):
- We must come out with a viable, reasonable and forward-looking science policy statement as well as a technology policy statement, and take steps to implement their provisions.
- The Scientific Advisory Committee to the Prime Minister must be reconstituted so that it delivers.
- We must exercise appropriate care in making appointments of heads of scientific agencies such as CSIR, and learn lessons from recent happenings in the Department of Space.
- The NAC (National Advisory Council, headed by Mrs Sonia Gandhi) must have at least two members with a background of S&T.
- Doordarshan should start (with Vignan Prasar) a science channel (available in all languages) which would also cover agriculture, health and environment.

(7) Creation of New States:
- A State Reorganization Commission should be formed with a mandate of working out criteria for division of states while keeping in mind the optimal limit of size for a state to be viable. It must give a report within six months, applying these criteria to all existing states, and suggesting division or reorganisation wherever considered advisable according to the above criteria.

(8) Agriculture and Rural Sector:
- Our research in agriculture must be directed towards self-reliance at the level of both farmer and country. Some areas where research should be encouraged would be: apomixis (which would make farmers independent of seed companies in regard to use of hybrids, and where we are a leader) and molecular breeding.

- GOI must examine (through appointment of a suitable group including NGOs and civil society) the reasons for over 2.6 lakh farmer suicides in the last dozen years or so, and come out with a white paper on it, stating clearly the steps it would take to prevent further suicides.
- There must be no indiscriminate support to GMOs. For example, we must first determine if there is a need for a GMO and, if so, are there better alternatives. If not, appropriate tests to ensure no adverse effect on human and animal health, soil, environment, biodiversity and sustainability, must be carried out by an independent organization set up for this purpose which will also do seed-testing using DNA fingerprinting. The proposed BRAI (Biotechnology Regulatory Authority of India) bill in this regard must be scrapped and replaced by an independent appropriate regulatory authority involving all stakeholders (for a critique of BRAI, see Appendix 6). For the time being, there should be at least a 15-year moratorium on field trials of GM crops, and labelling of any food product containing or derived from a GMO must be made mandatory. The report of the Standing Committee of Parliament on Agriculture on GM crops should be accepted by the Parliament and followed. India should also ratify the report of IAASTD (International Assessment of Agricultural Knowledge, Science and Technology for Development) and follow it.
- A reliable lab to test seeds as well as to conduct all required biosafety tests on GMOs and determine the presence of a GMO or GMO-derived material in a food product should be set up as has been also mentioned in the preceding section.
- The enormous potential of organic agriculture and agriculture using IPM (Integrated Pest Management) or NPM (Non-Pesticide Management) should be recognised and given appropriate support and encouragement.
- Recommendations (Appendix 7) of four meetings jointly chaired by DG, ICAR, and one of us (when he was the Vice-Chairman of NKC)

on Post-harvest Technologies, Organic Agriculture, Integrated Pest Management and Biopesticides, and Energy Use in Agriculture, should be implemented. The many success stories we have in these areas should be publicized. For example, in Andhra Pradesh, 3.7 million acres of agricultural land covering 11,000 villages is, most successfully, under NPM as of April 2013, making AP the only state where the use of pesticides has declined. Further, there have been no farmers' suicides where NPM has been used.

- ICAR must prepare a soil map of India and set up a system to keep it updated.
- We must create better and adequate decentralized storage facilities for grain.
- We must not permit any FDI in the seed sector.
- Fertilizer and power subsidy to the agriculture sector must be withdrawn. It should be replaced by instructions on judicious use of fertilizers, including organic fertilizers, and assured and quality power provided at the stipulated time.
- Connectivity to all our villages must be provided on a time-bound basis.
- Every village household should have workable access to functional toilets and basic sanitary facilities.
- The person who tills the land must have a stake in the land or the profit it brings.
- For successful implementation of NREGS, the employment must create tangible assets as per carefully prepared and viable development plans for the region. Further, it must be free of corruption.
- The enormous waste of grain (Appendix 8) and other food material must be avoided.

(9) Emphasis on Equity rather than Growth:

- The present emphasis on growth has brought very little benefit to the bottom 80 per cent of the population, though it has led to a substantial increase in the number of billionaires in India, and benefitted the top 20 per cent several orders of magnitude more than the bottom 80 per cent. Even in the top 20 per cent, the top 10 per cent have benefitted more than the bottom 10 per cent, and so on. As a consequence, the gap between the "rich" and the "poor" has been increasing, making a mockery of our being a "Socialist Republic". This must change in favour of improving the lot of the bottom 80 per cent. This change can happen only when the emphasis is not on growth of GDP but on growth of the bottom 80 per cent and, even there, greater emphasis on the bottom 40 per cent. In every step directed towards growth that we take, we must ask as to how it is going to affect the poorest of the poor. If we were to ask this question of ourselves, we would not even think of opening our retail sector to FDI.

- We must recognise the extent and importance of innovation in the organised sector and empower the National Innovation Foundation appropriately (say, through a one-time grant of Rs.1,000 crore) to commercialise such innovations.
- A system of social security (e.g. unemployment benefit) for the unorganised sector must be instituted.

(10) Police:

- We badly need police reforms that would bring about the much-needed change in the culture, ethos and performance of the police so that it can meet the expectations of our people, some of which are outlined in Appendix 9. To make this possible, an appropriate Commission on Police Reforms which would include respected members of civil society should be set up and asked to give its report in six months. This report should be put in the public domain and, after appropriate modifications, implemented within a year.
- One important step that would need to be taken is the professionalization within the police. Thus, an IPS officer who selects "traffic" at the time of his recruitment, and initial training

following the recruitment, must stay with "traffic" all through his career. This should not come in the way of his promotion. This would also be true of people down the line who are involved in management of traffic.

- The above-mentioned Commission should look into the role of today's police in crimes such as torture and rape about which we read virtually everyday in our newspapers. The Commission should ask why, according to NHRC, as of July 2012, there had been 16 fake encounters in two years in Andhra Pradesh, with no action taken against those responsible for these encounters. The recommendations of the Commission must be such that citizens can look up to police for help and protection as is the case, for example, in the UK.

(11) Tribals:

- PESA must be implemented both in spirit and in law.
- Similarly, the Forest Dwellers Rights Act (FRA) must also be implemented.
- Large numbers of tribals have been detained by the police in areas where Maoist (Left-Wing Extremist) activity is high. Several tribals also have cases registered against them which have no basis—e.g. "bind-over" cases in AP. There should be a commitment to effective legal aid and release of tribals caught in the cross-fire between Maoists and the police.
- The implementation of NREGS in tribal areas must be systematically audited and, where required, corrective measures taken.
- There should be a clear delineation of jurisdiction of the Forest Department in tribal areas after the enactment of FRA. This delineation should be clearly communicated to the Forest Department at all levels and the local administration. Currently, the Forest Department prevents the implementation of FRA, especially in interior tribal forest habitations.

- An appropriate land acquisition bill respecting the ethical, moral and legal rights of farmers, village dwellers and tribals should be passed and implemented.

(12) Municipal Administration:

- The government must recognize that in most places in the country such as Hyderabad, municipal administration is virtually non-existent. There is filth and garbage·all over in urban areas— excepting, perhaps, where the rich live. There are few footpaths, and the traffic is totally chaotic with unnecessary traffic jams. The present municipal administration engages in unnecessary and harmful mega projects, like the METRO in Hyderabad which has been opposed by every section of civil society and for extremely good reasons which have never been countered. The Government of Andhra Pradesh (as has been reported in the newspapers) has (as of July 2012) spent about Rs.5 crores per day as delay charges to L&T which has been given the contract.
- Again, the only way to take care of problems such as those mentioned above is to professionalise municipal administration from the top downwards, as is the case in most countries (such as the US) around the world.
- Municipal administration in urban areas should provide security against eviction to street vendors through provision for them of easily accessible designated areas with public facilities.
- Municipal administration must provide clean and safe public sanitation and drinking water to every resident in the area it administers.
- "Tragedy of the commons"—that is, privatization of land that is commonly used must be avoided.

(13) Electoral Reforms:

- There should be a provision for either proportional representation or requirement for 51% votes for someone to be elected.

- Anyone who has a prima facie criminal case pending against him/ her as adjudged by an independent judicial body of high public credibility for more than one year should not be allowed to contest an election. (As of 15th July, 2012, 31% of the Members of Parliament and State Legislature had criminal cases pending against them.)
- We need to set up stringent requirements to make a person eligible for election as a legislator or parliamentarian. We should remember that we have tests for selection almost everywhere else (for example, in our central services, and nationalized banks). Therefore, an appropriately designed test for a prospective legislator/ parliamentarian may not be out of place!
- There must be a provision in the law to recall publicly elected individuals.

(14) Scientific Temper and Secularism:

- The support of the government to religious practices and the involvement of government officials in such practices must be prohibited. It was shocking to see ISRO scientists taking a model of PSLV to a Hindu temple for obtaining the blessings of the deity for a successful launch on 9th September 2012. It was just as shocking to have a Hindu religious ceremony performed on 8th September 2012 when Air India took delivery of its new Boeing plane.
- The participation of top government officials selectively in religious ceremonies, such as the one in Puttaparthi following the death of the controversial Satya Sai Baba, is not in keeping with the spirit of secularism or scientific temper the country is constitutionally committed to. Another example would be the road-broadening activities in Hyderabad where a Christian shrine near Mettuguda has been shifted but a large Hindu temple set up right in the middle of the road and causing enormous traffic problems continues to be there, probably without any legal status.

- The support of the government to practices repeatedly proven as unscientific, such as astrology, must be withdrawn, while not interfering with the right of any individual to engage in any such unscientific practice as long as it does not come in the way of the rights of others.
- Keeping in mind the fact that certain festivals have come to have an increasing social significance relative to their religious significance, the government may consider declaring a number of such festivals as national festivals. Thus, Holi could be the festival of colour, Eid the festival of friendship, Diwali the festival of light, Dusserah or Durga Puja the festival of commitment to basic human values, and Christmas the festival of reiterating family ties.
- The government may consider declaring 2015 or 2016 as the Year of Scientific Temper. During this period, we may also do a survey of the extent of prevalence of scientific temper in the country.

(15) General Administration:

- We must analyse objectively the causes of the emergence of left-wing extremism and deal with them through a judicious combination of development, dialogue and discipline. The greatest mistake we can make is to treat those involved in left-wing extremist activity as ordinary criminals.
- India ranks 115 on women empowerment around the world—lower than 44 out of 54 African countries; each year there are some 1000 honour killings of our women. The administration must deal decisively and quickly with institutions such as Khap Panchayats and the process of Talibanisation of villages even close to Delhi.
- A system of financial, professional and social accountability at all levels of administration should be instituted and implemented. For example, the public has a right to know what has happened to the grant given by GOI to MP Government for taking care of Bhopal gas tragedy victims.

- Appropriate zoning laws should be passed and implemented.
- An appropriate system to screen hazardous technologies must be set up, recognizing that industrial pollution is among the top five causes of death in India. The Bhopal Gas Tragedy was a consequence of the lack of such a system. At least in two other cases, attempts by the US to impose such technologies on India were thwarted by the civil society. (P M Bhargava, "High stakes in agro research: Resisting the push", *Economic and Political Weekly*, August 23-29, 2003, vol. XXXVIII, no. 34, p.3537.)

(16) Traditional Knowledge and Resources:
- We must recognize that their optimum use can generate revenue of several hundred thousand crore rupees per year and provide employment (additional or full-time) to scores of millions of people in the country. An example will be the world-wide marketing of the unparalleled variety we have of vegetables and fruits—many with established useful pharmacological properties, as Sri Lanka has done with jackfruit (Appendix 10). The recommendations made in Appendix 11 in this regard may be followed.

(17) Environment:
- A National Environment Advisory Council consisting of well-known and respected environmentalists and scientists should be set up.

(18) Foreign Policy:
- The government must recognize that it is today largely perceived as being aligned with the USA and thus losing its independence. Such a perception, we must accept, is not without reason. Examples would be the Indo-US CEO Agreement to which the government seems to be committed; the Indo-US Knowledge Initiative in Agriculture; the reluctance on the part of the government to make DOW pay for the removal of the several hundred tonnes of toxic waste lying

on the surface in the Union Carbide factory in Bhopal and to de-toxify the soil and well water in the Union Carbide factory and the adjoining areas in Bhopal; the government's desire to permit FDI in retail sector; the vote against Iran's right to have its own nuclear programme; and our not pursuing the gas pipeline from Iran. Even our criticism of the US invasion of Iraq was highly muted. India's foreign policy must be directed towards asserting its independence and decision-making in all areas as was the case when India was a recognized leader of the Non-Aligned Movement in its hey-days.

- In the Islamic world, India must show a tilt towards non-Wahabi countries such as Jordan, recognizing that Islamic terrorism and fundamentalism are a corollary of the emergence and progression of the power of Wahabi groups.

Appendix 1

"The Right to Education Act: Is it right?"

P M Bhargava, *The Hindu*, 26th July 2010.

Something that cannot work, will not work. This is a tautology applicable to the Right to Education (RTE) Act which cannot meet the objectives for which it was set up for the following reasons.

The Act does not rule out education institutions set up for profit [Section 2.n.(iv)]. The protagonists of such institutions cite Article 19.1.g ("All citizens shall have the right to practice any profession or to carry out any occupation, trade or business.") in their support. However, they fail to recognize that the above article is regulated by Article 19.6; it is because of the provisions in Article 19.6 that no one in the country can set up a nuclear energy plant, or grow drugs, or build satellites, unless approved by the government. P N Bakshi (former member of the Law Commission) in his book on the Constitution of India says, "Education *per se* has so far not been regarded as a trade or business where profit is a motive". Yet, the TMA Pai Foundation vs Government of Karnataka judgement of the Supreme Court in 2003 said that it is difficult to comprehend that education per se will not fall under any of the four expressions in Article 19.1.g. Therefore, appropriately, model Rules and Regulations (R&R) for the RTE Act say in Section 11.1.b that a school run for profit by any individual, group or association of individuals or any other persons, shall not receive recognition from the government. However, this Section will not be binding on the states as it is not a part of the Act. If the GOI was serious about it, they should have made it a part of the RTE Act.

The common-sense resolution of the discrepancy between the above-mentioned Supreme Court judgement and the model R&R for the RTE Act could lie in the fact that education is a generic term. We need to distinguish between (a) the minimum quantum of education that a citizen should have to be able to discharge one's responsibilities and claim one's rights, and (b) subsequent education geared to train one for a profession such as medicine or engineering. As regards the first category, it is now virtually universally recognized that 12 years of school education beginning at the age of 6, preceded by appropriate pre-school education, is a minimum requirement. Therefore, in virtually all developed countries, a vast majority of children, including those of the rich and powerful, go to government schools for 12 years of totally free education. The RTE Act is unconcerned about the four most important years of school education—that is from Class IX to Class XII.

The second category would include three sub-categories: (a) higher education which could lead to a technical diploma, a first university degree in broad areas such as liberal arts, science or commerce, or post-graduate education in these areas; (b) education leading to a university degree, in a common profession of prime public interest that would cater to the basic needs of society, such as medicine, engineering, law, or management; and (c) education leading to training in highly specialized areas (which could vary with time), such as flying, catering or hotel management, which does not lead to a degree but is a prerequisite for joining the profession at an appropriate level.

It stands to common sense that the first category of education should be totally free with no hidden costs whatsoever. In the second category, in public interest, and to ensure that quality is maintained, the education in sub-categories (a) and (b) must be in a non-profit organization, the selections being made on merit in a means-independent way which would imply that appropriate fees could be charged from those who can pay; those who cannot pay must be able to continue their education through either freeships or scholarships, or a bank loan arranged by the institution.

There is no argument against education in sub-category (c) of the second category being provided for profit, for the employers will ensure quality in the institutions providing such education.

The judgement in the case of TMA Pai Foundation would appropriately apply to sub-category (c). There is, therefore, a strong case for ensuring that Section 11.1.b of the model R&R of the RTE Act is made mandatory for all schools without exception through an amendment of the Act.

The argument is that if people can pay for education of their children, they should have a right to have their own schools where the fee charged would be determined by them or the authorities of the school they set up. Indeed, according to our constitution we cannot ban such schools which will essentially be the *de facto* profitmaking schools of today where almost exclusively the children of the rich and powerful go. However, it is within the rights of the government to say that such schools would not be recognized as they would violate the principle of equity in regard to the minimum education that every citizen of India should have.

The RTE Act and its R&R fail on many other counts such as the following:

(a) Experience tells us that no government school is likely to function well (as well as the government schools did till about 1970) unless children of the rich and powerful also attend such schools. Further, it is a myth that private—*de facto* commercial—schools provide better training than, say, a Central School of the Government of India or trust-run schools which are truly not for profit.

(b) The Act places no restriction on the fees that may be charged by unaided private schools ostensibly set up as a Society or Trust but, *de facto*, set up to make money for the investors, just like a company. If they are truly set up not to make any profit they should not be charging any fees, and the fees paid by the children in the school should be reimbursed by the government. They could then function as a part of the common school system in which children of the neighbourhood would have to go irrespective of the class or status they belong to.

(c) Why should unaided private schools have a system of management with no obligatory participation of parents, unlike other schools that require the formation of a school management committee in which parents will constitute three-fourth of its membership?

(d) Why should there be a limit of only 25 per cent poor children in private unaided schools? Why not 10, 20, 40, 60 or 80 per cent? Wouldn't it create a divide among the children of the poor, leave aside a greater divide between the children of the rich and the poor?

(e) No method is prescribed for selecting the 25 per cent poor students for admission into unaided private schools. Selection by lottery would be ridiculous. In the absence of a viable provision, the private unaided (*de facto* commercial) schools can choose the 25 per cent poor children in a way that the choice would benefit only the school.

(f) There is nothing in the Act or its R&R which will prevent unaided private schools from charging the students for various activities that are not mentioned in the Act or its R&R. Examples would be laboratory fee; computer fee; building fee; sports fee; fee for stationary; fee for school uniform; fee for extra-curricular activities such as music, painting, pottery; and so on.

(g) Norms for building, number of working days, teacher workload, equipment, library and extra-curricular activities are prescribed only for unaided schools, and not for other schools including government schools. Only an obligatory teacher-student ratio is prescribed both for government and unaided schools. This means that as long as the teacher-pupil ratio is maintained, the school would be considered as fit. Thus, even if a government school has 12 students in each class from I to V, the school will have only two teachers!

(h) Two arguments often given for continuing to have, even encouraging, private unaided schools are that the government has no money to set up the needed schools, and that government schools cannot be run as well as private schools. Both these contentions are deliberate lies. There have been many excellent studies and reports that show that the government can find money to adopt a common school system with a provision of compulsory and totally free education upto Class XII in the country over the next 10 years. Further, even today the best system of school education in the country is the Central Schools system run by the government. The country needs 400,000 such schools and we *can* afford it.

The RTE Act and its R&R are destined not to work. We should recognize that if we do not take appropriate care of school education, agriculture and left-wing extremism—and all the three are related—we may very well be creating a condition that would encourage an internal revolution.

Appendix 2

The titles/salient features of some randomly selected newspaper reports on school education since the Right to Education Act was passed.

The Hindu: Hindu
The New Indian Express: NIE
The Times of India: TOI
Deccan Chronicle: DC

(only titles and sub-titles are given in most cases)

2010

1. Hindu. June 4, 2010

    The hidden costs of school education: Peer pressure and school rules for branded, fancy goods pinch parent's pockets.

2. DC. June 13, 2010

    Schools burn a hole in the pocket. As the new academic session begins from Monday, parents are trying to cope with the spiraling fees and fleecing by school managements.

3. NIE. June 13, 2010

    Children and the road to empowerment. After sixty-two years of Independence, India enacted a law that made education not just a right, but also compulsory and free – at least for eight academic years of a child's life. Now, a year later, we attempt to show you how the law will affect your life and how the initial euphoria or dismay has percolated into actions, responses and preparation. More importantly, we try to gauge whether free and compulsory education will ever truly become a universal right for our young.

4. Hindu. June 13, 2010

    Six-point action plan for schools in State. Chief Minister reviews issues related to education on the eve of the new academic year.

5. Hindu. June 18, 2010

   'Shocking' state of schools. An electric pole in the Sultan Bazaar Government School premises electrifies the walls whenever it rains!

6. NIE. June 18, 2010

   Corporate schools running unfit buses. 51 vehicles seized for not having fitness certificate.

7. DC. June 23, 2010

   14 score zero, pass Eamcet.

8. DC. July 9, 2010

   'Seat-for-sale' business picks up. With complete disregard to government norms, private colleges are selling management quota seats at a premium through brokers.

9. DC. July 11, 2010

   Private colleges flout fee norms. "Colleges demand extra money in the name of mess fees, bus fees or special fees," Parent.

10. TOI. August 28, 2010

    State can regulate private school fees: HC

11. DC. October 13, 2010

    AP tech graduates find no takers. A recent study has revealed that only 10 per cent of the state's engineering graduates are 'actually employable'. The major 'skill gap' has been blamed for the poor state of affairs.

12. DC. October 28, 2010

    College projects on sale for Rs.20k.

1. DC. January 3, 2011
    State turns its back on RTE. Although it has been eight months since the RTE came into force, the state is yet to implement it as schools flout norms and officials are still clueless about the Act's status.

2. DC. January 6, 2011
    Cutoff mark 50 for engineering.

3. NIE. January 15, 2011
    Parents make beeline to private schools.

4. DC. January 15, 2011
    Bihar makes significant all-round progress. School education quality has declined, says report.

5. DC. May 26, 2011
    Students buy projects from small IT firms for Rs.6-10 lakh. Most IT grads unemployable.

6. TOI. May 28, 2011
    Centre plans law to ban capitation fee in schools.

7. NIE. June 4, 2011
    'Schools cannot hike fees without consulting parents'.
    Recognition of a school to be cancelled if found collecting more fees than prescribed by the parents' committee.

8. NIE. June 9, 2011
    50,000 Engineering seats may remain vacant this year. 2.7 lakh seats are available and only 2.22 lakh candidates qualified in the Eamcet this year.

9. DC. July 27, 2011

   VC post: AP adopts 'local' policy. Despite spending exorbitantly on national notifications for VC posts, the state government sticks to local appointments, ignoring UGC rules and compromising on the quality of education.

10. Hindu. July 31, 2011

    Poor standard of results in JNTU. First-year students falter in engineering course; only 34.2 p.c. clear annual exam.

11. Hindu. August 15, 2011

    80,000 engineering, pharmacy seats vacant. After allotment, about 80,000 pharmacy, engineering seats vacant in convener quota.

12. TOI. December 18, 2011

    Caste pressures delay VC appointments.

2012

1. TOI. January 4, 2012

   AP in for education boom or bust? 6,761 new private junior colleges to come up in State.

2. DC. January 26, 2012

   CBI, MCI teams raid colleges.

3. TOI. January 13, 2012

   Politics at work in selection of UGC chairperson's post.

4. NIE. March 18, 2012

   Just 4 of 3,116 colleges reported it right on salaries.

5. Hindu. April 12, 2012
    Beyond the Right to Education lies a school of hard knocks.
    Euphoria over the Supreme Court's nod for the RTE Act could
    evaporate if we do some hard math.

6. Hindu. May 31, 2012
    Rising cost of education stifles parents. Many private schools
    stipulate that students buy textbooks, stationery from them.

7. NIE. August 18, 2012
    Labyrinth of Higher Education

2013

1. TOI. January 18, 2013
    Enrolment in private schools rise sharply in rural India.

2. TOI. January 19, 2013
    'Reading levels sink among 10-year-olds'.

3. NIE. February 2, 2013
    Only 10 pc MBAs of tier-2, 3 colleges get jobs

4. NIE. February 14, 2013
    Give Rs.200, pass Inter practicals! Some college managements ask
    students to cough up Rs.200-Rs.1,000 to bribe external examiners
    for getting good marks.

5. DC. February 19, 2013
    City schools keep fee a big secret. Parents unable to pick schools
    for kids.

Appendix 3

Some salient features of the report of the committee to Advise on Renovation and Rejuvenation of Higher Education, chaired by Prof. Yashpal, set up by Human Resource Development Minister.

SUMMARY OF MAJOR RECOMMENDATIONS

1. An all-encompassing National Commission for Higher Education and Research (NCHER), a constitutional body, should be created to replace the existing regulatory bodies such as the UGC and the AICTE, and the constitutional amendment followed up with an appropriate law for the Commission's functioning.

2. Universities should be made responsible regarding the academic content of all courses and programmes of study including professional courses. Professional bodies, like the AICTE and the MCI, to be divested of their academic functions, which would be restored to the universities.

3. Curricular reform must be the topmost priority of the newly-created NCHER which would create a curricular framework based on the principles of mobility within a full range of curricular areas, and integration of skills with academic depth.

4. It should be mandatory for all universities to have a rich undergraduate programme and undergraduate students must get opportunities to interact with the best faculty. While appointing teachers to the universities, their affiliation to a particular college should also be specified to emphasize the need for their exposure to undergraduate students.

5. Undergraduate programmes should be restructured to enable students to have opportunities to access all curricular areas with fair degree of mobility. It is highly recommended that, normally, no single discipline or specialized university should be created.

6. The vocational education sector is at present outside the purview of universities and colleges. Alienation of this sector can be overcome by bringing it under the purview of universities and by providing necessary accreditation to the courses available in polytechnics, industrial training institutions, and so on. Additionally, the barriers to entry into universities for students going through vocational training should be lowered to enable them to upgrade their knowledge base at any stage of their career.

7. The NCHER should also galvanize research in the university system through the creation of a National Research Foundation.

8. New governing structures should be evolved to enable the universities to preserve their autonomy in a transparent and accountable manner.

9. The practice of according the status of deemed university should be stopped forthwith till the NCHER takes a considered view on it. It would be mandatory for all existing deemed universities to submit to the new accreditation norms to be framed on the lines proposed in the report within a period of three years, failing which the status of a university should be withdrawn. However, unique educational initiatives which have over a period of time enriched higher education by their innovations should be given recognition and supported appropriately.

10. Modern higher education system requires extension facilities, sophisticated equipment and highly specialized knowledge and competent teachers. It would not be possible for every university to

possess the best of these infrastructures. Hence, one of the primary tasks of the NCHER should be to create several inter-university centres (IUCs) in diverse fields to create the best of these possibilities and attract the participation of several institutions of higher learning to avail them. This model has already been successfully demonstrated by the IUCs of the UGC like the Inter University Centre for Astronomy and Astrophysics, and the Inter University Accelerator Centre.

11. Institutions of excellence like the IITs and IIMs should be encouraged to diversify and expand their scope to work as full-fledged universities, while keeping intact their unique features, which shall act as pace-setters and model governance systems for all universities.

12. One of the first tasks of the NCHER should be to identify the best 1,500 colleges across India to upgrade them as universities, and create clusters of other potentially good colleges to evolve as universities.

13. Universities should establish a live relationship with the real world outside and develop capacities to respond to the challenges faced by rural and urban economies and culture.

14. All levels of teacher education should be brought under the purview of higher education.

15. A national testing scheme for admission to the universities on the pattern of the GRE should be evolved which would be open to all the aspirants of University education, and held more than once a year. Students would be permitted to send their best test score to the universities of their choice.

16. Quantum of Central financial support to state-funded universities should be enhanced substantially on an incentive pattern, keeping in view the need for their growth.

17. Expansion of the higher education system should be evaluated and assessed continuously to excel and to respond to the needs of different regions in India in order to ensure not only equity and access but also quality and opportunity of growth along the academic vertical. The NCHER too should be subject to external review once in five years.

18. A National Education Tribunal should be established with powers to adjudicate on disputes among stakeholders within institutions and between institutions so as to reduce litigation in courts involving universities and higher education institutions.

19. A Task Force should be set up to follow up on the implementation of this Agenda for action within a definite time-frame.

Some of these recommendations may be implemented immediately while others may take some evolutionary steps and procedures. Even so, it is hoped that the ideas behind them would be kept alive by keeping them under active and wide-ranging discussion. In fact, there should be an educational movement to continuously articulate and debate these issues so that changes are made in keeping with the emerging trends nationally and globally in regard to the most effective forms of higher education.

These recommendations are not for all times to come. There should be sufficient social and political awareness to continuously monitor and adopt new innovations based on the ever-evolving demands of the society and economy.

Appendix 4

Recommendations of the UGC in regard to collaboration of Indian universities with universities abroad.

The UGC has come out with regulations to ensure academic collaboration between Indian and foreign institutions. The regulations titled the UGC (Promotion and maintenance of standards of academic collaboration between Indian and foreign educational institutions) Regulations, 2012, are yet to be notified.

These regulations shall come into force from the date of notification in the Official Gazette. They shall apply to all Foreign Educational Institutions (FEIs) operating in India through collaboration with Indian Educational Institutions (IEIs) other than technical institutions or IEIs operating through collaboration with FEIs for offering their programmes leading to award of degrees / PG diplomas. It will apply to all the institutions operating either prior to the coming into force of these regulations, or intending to operate through collaboration, for offering their programmes leading to award of degrees / PG diplomas.

Any IEI or FEI already having a collaborative arrangement shall comply with these regulations within one year from the date of their coming into force.

Eligibility Criteria
FEIs collaborating with IEIs shall satisfy the following criteria / conditions:

- FEI shall have been ranked among the best 500 institutions in the world by an internationally acknowledged ranking system.
- FEI shall have operative arrangements in India through IEI.
- FEI shall ensure that all the programmes offered by it are in conformity with the standards laid down by the statutory body concerned.
- FEI shall abide by all the conditions prescribed by the GOI / statutory bodies from time to time.

IEIs collaborating with FEIs shall satisfy the following criteria / conditions:

- At the time of agreement for collaboration, the IEI shall have accreditation by NAAC with a grade not less than B or its equivalent.
- The IEI shall have experience of 5 years in offering educational services at the level of degree / PG diploma.
- The IEI's academic and other infrastructure shall meet the requirements stipulated by the concerned statutory body.
- If the IEI concerned is an affiliated institution, it shall obtain prior approval from the affiliating university for entering into collaboration with an FEI.

All institutions (FEIs / IEIs) involved in collaborative, twinning or other forms of partnership arrangements shall satisfy the following criteria / conditions:

1. Academic requirements and other details of the programmes of study shall be made public before the commencement of the programme by the IEI concerned.
2. No programme of study / research shall be offered which jeopardizes national security and territorial integrity of India.
3. The IEI concerned shall abide by any other conditions prescribed by GOI or statutory body concerned from time to time.
4. In the matters of foreign exchange all the institutions concerned shall abide by the norms / regulations of the RBI / GOI.

Procedure for collaboration
1. FEIs collaborating with IEIs shall obtain an NOC from MHRD.
2. FEIs collaborating with IEIs shall have to enter into a written agreement / MoU with the IEIs and a copy of the same shall be forwarded to the Commission. The same shall also be uploaded on its/their website(s).

Consequences of violation

1. The Commission either on its own or on the basis of any complaint may cause an inquiry, including physical inspection. If satisfied that the collaborating institution(s) is/are not functioning in accordance with these regulations, it may issue directions for termination of the agreement / MoU for collaboration.

   Before issuing directions for termination, the institution concerned shall be given an opportunity to explain its position.

2. In case of violation of these regulations by the institution, the Commission shall notify the same on its website and also through media that the programmes offered / conducted through the collaborative arrangements are not in conformity with the regulations.

3. Appropriate action may also be taken against IEIs as deemed fit and proper by the Commission.

Interpretation

1. Decision of the Commission shall be final in regard to the issue of interpretation of the regulations.
2. Commission shall have the power to issue clarifications in regard to the implementation of these regulations.
3. All disputes arising in relation to collaborative arrangement between an IEI and an FEI shall be governed by Indian law.

Appendix 5

"Take this patient to ICU" (A cure for India's healthcare ills is within reach provided there is political will), P M Bhargava,
The Hindu, 14th July 2012.

In most developed—and many developing—countries today, a 12-year school education and universal health coverage (UHC) are the two primary responsibilities of the State. India has failed miserably on both counts. Let us look at some of the problems of medical and healthcare (medicare).

Fifty years ago, when there was no commercialisation of medicare that we have today, we had only government hospitals or those run by trusts as public service. There weren't enough of them but they provided excellent medicare by dedicated professionals. Today, the government hospitals are in shambles.

Medicare of reasonable quality is currently largely commercialized and corporatized, the primary objective being to get the maximum money from patients by giving them the minimum possible in return. The irony is that while the average quality of healthcare provided by commercial hospitals is far from satisfactory, we have in them, taken altogether, world-class expertise in virtually every field of medicare. Therefore, you can get the best possible medical attention in our country if you have unlimited money.

Many commercial hospitals in the country have been given land at concessional rates and exemption of duty on imported equipment on the condition that they would treat a certain percentage of poor people for free. However, there may not be even one hospital that meets this obligation.

Quality of education

The quality of medical education—barring in a handful of elite institutions —has progressively gone down. Till recently, recognition by the Medical Council of India (MCI), the accrediting body for medical colleges, was based not on the ability of the proposed institution to provide quality education but its ability to pay the Chairman of MCI (one of whom has been jailed) and members of the inspection team. This expense was more than recovered by the capitation fee charged for admission in the medical college, and a guaranteed degree irrespective of ability or performance.

The system of general physicians (GPs), which is the backbone of the National Health Service in the United Kingdom that provides one of the best UHC in the world and which was also the backbone of our medicare system when we became Independent, has virtually disappeared. Till recently, no medical college provided an MD course in family medicine. After I gave the convocation address at the West Bengal University of Health Sciences a few years ago, the Government of West Bengal, with the support of Gopal Gandhi, then Governor of the State, his Health Minister, and the University Vice-Chancellor, decided to introduce an MD course in family medicine. This may, however, be the only one of its kind.

Consequently, today, it is the (often ignorant) patient who decides which specialist to go to, even for the most trivial of problems. Specialists, in most cases, in the private, commercial sector, find a disease of their specialty, even when it does not exist. Moreover, they are generally too busy to ask the patient if s/he has any other problem or is taking any other drug besides that prescribed by the specialist. We, thus, had a case in Hyderabad when a person chose to go to seven specialists, each one of whom prescribed him a course of antibiotics, he returned to the hospital as a victim of antibiotic toxicity. The fact is, unlike a specialist, a family physician (a GP) cannot recover the astronomical amount spent on getting admission to a medical college.

Many private commercial healthcare establishments have touts in villages who bring them patients against a commission. This was once recorded in a sting operation in Hyderabad and reported by us to the State Medical Council that did nothing about it.

Unnecessary diagnostic tests (for prescribing which a doctor gets commission from the diagnostic laboratory), surgical procedures and stay in the hospital are common practices resorted to by commercial hospitals.

Payoffs to doctors for recommending a particular test to be done in a particular diagnostic centre, or for recommending another doctor or hospital, are rampant.

There are also payoffs today to doctors in private hospitals. For example, in a private hospital in Bhopal that was ostensibly set up to take care of the gas disaster victims, Rs.2.81 crore was paid by the then hospital administration to 30 doctors in the hospital over and above their salary which was substantial, between 24th July, 2010 and 31st October, 2010, out of the money received from private patients, according to the data provided by the hospital itself under the RTI Act.

Neither fair nor transparent

The billing of patients in private hospitals is often neither fair nor transparent. I had the personal experience of having a bill presented to me at the time of getting my wife discharged from a corporate hospital in Hyderabad, in which the charges for anaesthesia (couched in a language that did not make sense) were included even though my wife was not administered any anaesthesia.

The right of the patient to have a copy of his medical record is often not respected.

There is no legal imperative today for a hospital, diagnostic centre, or infertility clinic, to be registered and accredited. Through the efforts of The MARCH (The Medically Aware and Responsible Citizens of Hyderabad), an organisation which has met every month in Hyderabad since September

1995, our country has a system of voluntary accreditation of clinical laboratories, this must be made mandatory. Similarly, through another initiative taken by The MARCH nearly a decade ago, we today have a bill for accreditation and supervision of infertility clinics ready to be placed before Parliament. None of the problems, for example, relating to surrogacy, that we have been reading in the press recently, would have arisen if the provisions of the bill had been followed. And very few hospitals in the country are accredited under the National Accreditation Board for Hospitals as such accreditation is voluntary.

It appears that 10–25 per cent of the drugs in the market are spurious or of low quality. The sources of such drugs are often known but nothing is done about them.

There is a nexus between drug companies and doctors who benefit substantially in cash or kind for prescribing a drug made by a particular company, even when cheaper or better alternatives are available.

There is no obligatory requirement for all registered medical practitioners to go through continuing medical education course (CMEs) to keep themselves updated in their area of expertise.

The course we used to have on medical ethics in our medical colleges has been abandoned. Therefore, ethics is not a word in the dictionary of most of our doctors.

We need an appropriate code for medical shops which, for example, should not be allowed to sell scheduled drugs without a prescription.

Terminally ill patients should be allowed to die in peace with as much comfort as possible. There are very few establishments in the country for palliative care of such patients.

Many of the clinical trials in this country ignore the ethical code—even the legal requirements—for clinical trials for which India is a key destination world-wide.

There is virtually no impartial market surveillance after the release of a new drug.

The consequence is that India is the world capital of malnutrition, stunted growth, infant and child mortality, burden of disease, and indebtedness on account of (often futile) out-of-pocket expenses on healthcare. A fair proportion of farmer suicides in the country out of over 250,000 during the last decade or so have been on account of inability to pay money borrowed at exorbitant rates of interest for healthcare.

The solutions to the problems mentioned above are obvious and well within our capabilities and resources if we have the political will. For example, the implementation of the excellent report (*The Hindu*, April 14, 2012) of the High Level Expert Group set up by the Planning Commission for working out modalities of UHC, under the Chairmanship of Dr K Srinath Reddy, will take care of several major problems mentioned above. Dr K K Talwar, present Chairman of the MCI and president of the National Academy of Medical Sciences, recently set up a high-power committee under the chairmanship of Dr Nirmal Ganguly (former Director-General of ICMR) to work out a code of ethics for medicare establishments and related organisations. We hope that the report of this committee will give us a framework for solving many other problems that have an ethical angle to them.

Appendix 6

"Unconstitutional, unethical, unscientific" (Problems with the Biotechnology Regulatory Authority of India Bill), P M Bhargava, *The Hindu*, 28th December 2011.

It is now widely accepted that the existing procedure in the country (even elsewhere) for the regulation of genetic engineering technology is faulty and insufficient. It was for this reason that Jairam Ramesh, former Minister for Environment and Forests, put an indefinite moratorium on the open release of genetically engineered Bt-brinjal which was approved by the Genetic Engineering Approval Committee of the above ministry on 14th October 2009.

The Biotechnology Regulatory Authority of India (BRAI) Bill that is proposed to be put up to the Parliament for approval claims to take care of the deficiencies in the present system of approval of genetically modified (GM) crops. As it turns out, the Bill is unconstitutional, unethical, unscientific, self-contradictory, and not people-oriented. It suffers from greater flaws and deficiencies than the present system. If passed, it will seriously and adversely affect agriculture, health of humans and animals, and the environment, causing unparalleled harm. I give below some reasons in support of the above view.

The BRAI will consist of three full-time and two part-time members. It will have three divisions, each headed by a Chief Regulatory Officer. The BRAI will be supported by a Risk Assessment Unit, an Enforcement Unit, a Monitoring Office, a Product Ruling Committee, an Environmental Appraisal Panel, Scientific Advisory Panels, an Inter-ministerial Governing Board, a Biotechnology Advisory Council, and State Biotechnology Regulatory Advisory Committees. The above bodies would consist mostly of bureaucrats who are likely to have little knowledge of the highly complex issues that arise in today's biotechnology. There is no civil society participation proposed anywhere. Even the proposed Biotechnology Regulatory Appellate Tribunal will not accept complaints from the civil society, in spite of the fact that the Bill will directly or indirectly affect every citizen of India. It is not even clear as to which department of the Government of India will service BRAI. The Convener of the Selection

Committee for members of the BRAI will be from the Department of Biotechnology (DBT) which is a vendor of genetic engineering (the technology that BRAI is supposed to regulate) in the country. The Bill says that the members of BRAI will be persons of integrity. There is, however, no requirement of integrity for members of any of the other committees mentioned above!

The Bill is unconstitutional as agriculture is a state subject, and the Bill takes away the authority to take decisions about GM plant products from the state governments. In this connection it is noteworthy that more than 10 states, cutting across all political affiliations, had formally told Jairam Ramesh in 2009-2010 that they will not permit Bt-brinjal to be released in their state.

Article 28 of the Bill states that the information declared by BRAI as "confidential commercial information" will not come under the RTI Act, and that there is no way that civil society can challenge the decision of BRAI to declare any information as confidential. In spite of the fact that BRAI encompasses activities that would virtually affect every Indian, there is no mention in the Bill of public consultation.

Articles 81, 86 and 87.2, which allow BRAI to override any existing law in the areas covered by BRAI, contradict Article 86 which says "the provisions (of BRAI) shall be in addition to, and not in derogation of, any other law for the time being in force".

The definition of modern biotechnology in Article 3 (r) is absurd as it excludes a large number (over 25) of areas such as peptide synthesis, immunotechnology, tissue culture, stem cells and nanobiotechnology that are integral part of today's biotechnology. Not only that, it would make techniques that are used in everyday research in modern biology such as isolation or sequencing of DNA and the PCR technique, illegal, unless approved by BRAI in every specific case. So every university in the country teaching these extremely widely used techniques will have to get permission from BRAI for teaching them to the students of BSc or MSc courses.

Even more funny is the inclusion in Schedule I (which lists organisms and products "which should be regulated by the Authority") of cloned animals, DNA vaccines, and stem cells-based products. There is no mention of them in the main text of the Bill. Schedule I also includes "products of synthetic biology for human or animal use". I have been in the business of modern biology for six decades and seen the modern biological evolution from very close quarters with more than 20 of my friends having won Nobel prizes but, for the life of me, I cannot make out what is meant by "products of synthetic biology".

In fact, if one strictly followed item 2(d) of Schedule I, no organ transplantation will be possible in the country without permission from BRAI!

One would have also expected, if the Bill was people-oriented, for it to state the procedure to be adopted before approval of a GM product. The first step of this procedure should be to determine the need for the product through a socio-economic survey and analysis. If there is a need, then one should determine if there are cheaper, better and well-established alternatives such as smart or molecular breeding, organic agriculture, or use of Integrated Pest Management or biopesticides in the case of GM products containing a foreign pesticidal gene. If it is concluded that there is no alternative to a GM crop, then one would need to state a mechanism for deciding what the tests would be that the GM crop would need to undergo, and a statement of who will do the tests to ensure public credibility. There is no provision in the Bill for an independent testing laboratory for GM crops in which civil society would have confidence.

There is no mention of mandatory labelling of GM food products, and there is no protection provided to, say, farmers whose fields growing, for example products of organic agriculture, get contaminated by a GM product of the neighbouring farm.

Article 62 under "Offences and Penalties" is, as far as I know, unprecedented. It implies that if anyone makes a statement about a GM crop which BRAI decides is false or misleading, s/he shall be punishable with imprisonment for a term which may extend to three months and also with fine which may extend to Rs.5 lakh. BRAI will not be obliged to state the basis of its decision which will not be challengeable by any member of the civil society. The Bill thus assumes that all the wisdom regarding biotechnology lies with the five members of the Authority, and what thousands of leading scientists may say will cut no ice with the members of BRAI.

One may justifiably ask as to why this Bill. The reasons are clear. Food business is the biggest business in the world. Whosoever controls it would control the world. To control food production, one needs to control just seed and agrochemicals production. This is what a handful of multinational seed companies, who also are producers of agrochemicals such as pesticides and weedicides, are attempting to do through patented GM crops. These companies are located in the United States (US), and liaison closely with the Government of US.

In fact, one of the biggest quarrel between the US and Europe is that Europe, by and large, does not allow GM crops and requires appropriate labelling of all food products that contain more than 0.9 per cent of GM material. No such labelling is required in the US where, therefore, a person today does not know if he is consuming GM food.

Till a few years ago, there was no significant opposition to GM crops in India. In fact, the mechanism set up by the Government of India, ostensibly to regulate GM products, largely worked as a vendor of GM products, serving the interests of seed and agrochemical MNCs.

But then people of India became wiser and better-informed. Consequently, against all odds and expectations of the MNCs, and of the US Government and the rulers in India, we had an indefinite moratorium on Bt-brinjal, and the opposition to GM crops became a force to reckon with. Some components of the existing regulatory system have also begun to assert themselves. As of today, at least five states (Bihar, Madhya Pradesh, Kerala, Karnataka and Himachal Pradesh) have formally declared that they will not allow field trials and/or open release of any GM crop in their state. So, the present system had to be disabled, and road-blocks to fulfilling the ambition of the US and the seed MNCs removed. What better way to achieve this than BRAI—so the Government thought. But, I believe, GOI has again underestimated the collective wisdom of the people of India!

Appendix 7

A letter to the Prime Minister attaching reports of meetings under the auspices of ICAR on Post-Harvest Technology, Integrated Pest Management and Biopesticides, Organic Agriculture, and Energy Use in Agriculture.

May 9, 2007

Dr Manmohan Singh
Prime Minister of India
7, Race Course Road
New Delhi 110011

My dear Prime Minister,

Soon after the National Knowledge Commission (NKC) was formally inaugurated by you, we all had agreed that we must look at areas where knowledge input in agriculture can help transform it. We identified 21 areas where either existing knowledge has not been transmitted to the agriculture sector, or where new knowledge needs to be generated. These areas that were approved by the NKC are listed in Annexure 1.

Following my close association with the ICAR (Indian Council of Agricultural Research) for over four decades, I spoke to Dr Mangala Rai, Director General, ICAR, about the areas listed in Annexure 1. A visionary that he is, he agreed that we need to have meetings in each one of these areas to determine what the ICAR and the country may do to help our agriculture and rural sector. Subsequently, the following four meetings were organized by the ICAR, each one of them having been attended by 20-60 people, including representatives of every concerned sector:

[1]. Meeting on post-harvest technologies for value addition and income and employment generation, held in Bhopal at the Central Institute of Agriculture Engineering, on 2nd December 2005.

[2]. Brainstorming dialogue on organic farming organized by the Central Institute for Sub-tropical Horticulture, at the Indian Institute for Sugarcane Research at Lucknow, on 2nd February 2006.

[3]. Meeting on integrated pest management and biopesticides held at the National Academy of Agricultural Sciences in New Delhi, on 26th April 2006.

[4]. Brainstorming session on energy management in agriculture held at VPKAS (a laboratory of the ICAR) at Almora, on 29th May 2006.

I am enclosing the minutes of these meetings as Annexures 2, 3, 4 and 5 respectively.

I believe that action as recommended in the minutes of the above four meetings could help transform our agriculture substantially. It was unfortunate that agriculture had a backseat in the NKC as far as the other members of the NKC were concerned, and in spite of my repeated requests, no action was taken on the minutes of the above meetings, the first of which was held more than one-and-a-half years ago and the last of which was held a year ago. On account of lack of action on part of the NKC, the ICAR has also lost interest and no further meetings have been held on the remaining areas of Annexure 1.

The major recommendations of these meetings are as follows:

- The Government should set up a mission on Post-Harvest Technologies of which the objectives, goals and terms of reference are given in Annexure 2. An important recommendation is that the first step in post-harvest processing should be taken by the primary producer and that he must continue to be a stake-holder in all subsequent steps including marketing.
- A new institutional mechanism (perhaps a corporation or a cooperative) should be set up to encourage Organic Farming through appropriate mechanisms.
- The ICAR should set up a separate institute as a national centre for research and development in Organic Agriculture. Alternatively, the ICAR could convert one of its existing institutes to an institute devoted to Organic Agriculture.
- The Government should set up a group to define standards for products of Organic Agriculture, for domestic market labelling.
- Standard Operative Procedures should be prepared for Integrated Pest Management (IPM), which would drastically reduce the use

of synthetic pesticides and thus contamination of soil and ground-water), for various crops in all Schedule VIII languages.

- The ICAR should set up a National Quality Control Laboratory for materials used in IPM.
- A strategy for dissemination of procedures of IPM should be worked out (components of this strategy have been outlined in the report).
- An industrial set-up should be put in place, through an initiative of the ICAR, to produce various requirements for IPM.
- An appropriate number of ITIs should be set up for training in IPM at various levels, some within the ICAR system itself.
- The nine new energy saving technologies developed by the ICAR so far should be promoted through an appropriate mechanism.
- The National Energy Policy should include energy generation from surplus biomass and crop residue, for the exploitation of which an appropriate consortium should be set up.
- The importance of continued use of biomass, such as firewood, in the rural sector must be recognized and mechanisms for increasing the efficiency and convenience of such use (such as smokeless *chulah*s), and propagating them should be worked out.
- A well thought-out programme of energy plantations (social forestry) should be implemented.
- A revolving fund for entrepreneurs (with a corpus of say Rs.1,000 crores) should be set up for community biogas plants.
- Animal husbandry, fisheries, agriculture, fertilizers and other agro-chemicals, should be brought under a single department of the government.

I am taking the liberty of sending these recommendations to you as I believe they are important for the country and it is unlikely that they will come to you from the NKC. I hope you would find them of some value.

I am also enclosing (Annexure 6) three letters from Dr M S Swaminathan whom we had consulted on behalf of the NKC, in which he has said that all these recommendations should be forwarded to you. The NKC also ignored this letter!

The meeting reports in Annexures 2, 3 and 4 were prepared by me and my colleague, Mrs Chandana Chakrabarti, while the report of the meeting on energy use in agriculture (Annexure 5) was prepared by Dr Nawab Ali, Deputy Director-General, ICAR. May I also add, to be fair, that all the other reports that I have sent you were also prepared jointly by Chandana Chakrabarti and me. You would recall her as the co-author of the Agenda for the Nation that, with your encouragement, we had presented at 10, Janpath on 29th December 2003. I had persuaded her to devote two-third of her time to NKC, and she was appointed as a Research Associate after all the members of the NKC had met her and approved her appointment. She was the most experienced, in fact, the only truly experienced person, amongst the nearly 10 Research Associates who were appointed by the NKC from time to time – and the only member of the staff (including Advisers) who was appointed with the approval of all the members of the NKC, her experience covering almost all the areas with which the NKC has professed to be concerned. Her contribution to the NKC during the 20 months of her service was outstanding, and, I dare say, perhaps an order of magnitude greater, both in quality and in quantity, than that of any other Research Associate or Adviser. Yet she was the only one whose services were terminated on 31st March 2007, without giving any reason. The reasons that were provided to me by two persons in the office of the NKC were both different and hilariously absurd. This has been yet another example of the arbitrary functioning of the NKC.

With warm personal regards,

Yours sincerely,

Sd/-

(P M Bhargava)

Research Needs of Farmers

The following topics (randomly arranged) that relate to the felt needs of farmers are suggested for further research by ICAR and other organizations:

1. Post-harvest technology including technologies for value addition, such as food processing.
2. Water harvesting using traditional technologies.
3. New agriculture-product storage technologies, particularly for decentralized storage.
4. Veterinary genetics and pathology (including microbiology and virology), for example, sequencing of genomes of animals specially widely used in India, such as buffaloes; and developing genetically engineered vaccines for diseases such as FMV and rinderpest.
5. Organic agriculture and associated activities such as vermiculture.
6. Developing methodologies for quick marker-aided selection.
7. Integrated pest management: to increase experience and range of application and modification where necessary.
8. Introduction of hybrid vigour into pure-breeding varieties.
9. Setting up of commercial DNA fingerprinting of plants and seeds. Also documentation to help farmers ensure that they do not get spurious seeds.
10. Development of osmo-resistant varieties (MSSRF;CCMB), and encouragement of commercial plant tissue culture for producing products such as vanillin.
11. Better weather prediction models (DST;MST Radar Facility at Tirupati, of the Department of Space).
12. Identification of varieties of medicinal plants that would have high amounts of markers correlated with activity.
13. Development of technologies for use of agricultural waste products.

14. Technologies that could increase productivity and release time, labour and resources of farmers which could be utilized for additional employment.
15. Identification of avenues for additional employment and research on making them attractive and lucrative enough for farmers to engage in them.
16. A socio-economic analysis of the use of energy in agriculture, along with energy saving mechanisms and strategies for energy management.
17. Development and propagation of technologies for controlled release of fertilizers and pesticides.
18. Systems approach towards commercialization of existing technologies such as for orchid tissue culture in Arunachal Pradesh.
19. Metabolic engineering to generate more value (e.g. transferring genes of maize for enzymes, such as phosphoenol pyruvate carboxylasc/oxygenase and orthophosphate dikinase into rice for increasing yield).
20. An in-depth study of 'shifting agricultural practices', for example, in Arunachal Pradesh, to increase its efficiency.
21. Setting up a system for validating (or otherwise) traditional agricultural practices on which considerable documentation is available, e.g. with Anil Gupta of Ahmedabad.

These areas (as already mentioned in Annexure 2 of Part III) should be pursued by carefully selected, competent and committed scientists in a mission mode, with clear time-targets, appropriate funding based on milestones, freedom from bureaucratic hassles but professional, social and financial accountability.

First Consultative Meeting on Research Needs of Farmers

Post-Harvest Technologies for Value Addition, Income and Employment Generation

2nd December 2005

Central Institute of Agricultural Engineering (ICAR) Bhopal

Participants (about 40)

DG, ICAR (Dr Mangala Rai)

ICAR Scientists

Forest Department Officials (Government of Madhya Pradesh)

Agricultural Scientists (Government of Madhya Pradesh)

Farmers

Entrepreneurs

NGOs

P M Bhargava, Vice-Chairman, National Knowledge Commission (NKC)

Chandana Chakrabarti, NKC

At the meeting in Bhopal on 2nd December 2005, it was decided to recommend to the Government of India (GOI) that it may set up a mission on post-harvest technologies, of which the details are now given. The mission's target of value addition at the end of the third year should be Rs.10,000 crores, with a potential in the future of ten times this amount. If successful, the mission should be converted into a permanent council.

Mission on Post-Harvest Technologies

Objectives

Develop where necessary, communicate and ensure appropriate use of post-harvest technologies for optimal utilization of products and potential in the agricultural sector.

Goals

Enhanced income of rural communities

Employment generation

To help increase the contribution of agriculture to GDP from the present less than 20% to nearly 40%

Terms of reference

1. To collect, generate (where missing), collate and document (in English and eventually in Indian languages) the following information (as relevant) on agricultural and animal produce mentioned subsequently.

   Information required:
   - Varieties in use
   - Grown where in India (maps)?
   - Nutrient, including micronutrient, requirement
   - Evidence, if any, of lack of adequate nutrients
   - Climatic and soil requirement
   - Indicators for harvesting
   - Appropriate method of handling, from harvesting to processing, including storage (radiation sterilization where possible)
   - Processing technology: available or to be developed?
   - Nature of the end-product(s)
   - Chemistry, nutritive value and use(s) of the end product

Agricultural produce for which the above information should be put together:

- Cereals and spices
- Pulses
- Tea and coffee
- Oilseeds and nuts
- Fruits
- Vegetables
- Animal produce
- Poultry and eggs
- Natural fibre and timber
- Minor forest produce

2. To set phytosanitary standards and prepare SOPs for the various steps mentioned above, as appropriate to the product/produce.

3. To recommend to the GOI steps that may be taken to ensure that "Standard Setting Exercises" for the above under the auspices of the WTO do not lead to unfair protective barriers. On the other hand, we must ensure that the international standards agreed to would permit India-specific processes/materials (such as non-toxic vegetable colours) in respect of our agro-products.

4. To ensure connectivity (for example, roads), the necessary power (local power generation, e.g. by wind or a microhydel plant; adequate and quality power—not free power) and soil supplementation or treatment, wherever required.

5. To decentralize storage (even for buffer stock—thus dismantling FCI) and appropriately segregate produce/products to ensure no mix up of varieties or non-identical products.

6. To work out a policy of processing with emphasis on at least the first–stage processing to be done in the catchment area, in the small-scale sector, involving the primary producers.

7. To adopt a three-tier strategy (the first being what is mentioned above) for processing and marketing.

8. To define clearly and unambiguously a strategy for fair sharing of profits by all contributors on an equitable basis.

9. To ensure segregated marketing so that the source of each item can be traced. As far as possible, farmers should manage all the three tiers and thus have direct market access. If this is not possible, they should have a stake in the product being marketed (for example, through shares) given to them as producers.

10. To work out strategies for and identify parties (farmers, farmers' cooperatives, SMEs in the private or public/joint sector, larger industries with international marketing capability) who will be partners in processing, keeping in mind what is mentioned in (8) and (9) above.

11. To appropriately train the labour involved in the entire chain from plucking to preparing for the market. The training should be provided by the top-tier industrial set-up.

12. To develop and disseminate appropriate information packages for farmers, for both general and immediately relevant knowledge.

13. To set up ITIs that would provide training in post-harvest technologies and other items mentioned above to those who are (as appropriate) high-school fail, high-school pass, intermediate pass, or holding a degree.

14. To devise marketing strategies: for example, adequate publicity, meetings with ITDC and Hotels Association of India, for making them aware of the enormous variety in regard to vegetables and fruits in India which they can market; use of Embassies and

Departments of Tourism; production of easily readable books; setting up a website for Indian recipes to which any citizen can contribute free of cost and, similarly, any citizen can verify or comment on the contributed recipes; television programmes; exhibitions, to name a few.

15. To work out a system of relating subsidies to quantifiable parameters such as provision of micronutrients.

16. To set up our own quality standards in regard to every product, which should be sufficiently stringent but fair and implementable.

17. To help develop appropriate farm equipment and implements suitable for use by women, because of gender shift in agriculture on account of migration of men to cities.

18. To work out and implement a scheme of voluntary clubbing of villages for processing and marketing of value-added agro-products.

19. To set up a system for providing real-time information to farmers in various areas relevant to them such as weather.

20. To develop protocols for transportation of the primary produce at various stages, all the way to the market.

21. To ensure that the products satisfy international standards in regard to pesticidal contamination etc.; encourage use of bio-pesticides.

22. To install a suitable system for providing in real time (through NRSA) information on the best-sowing date.

23. To identify and set up entrepreneurs for manufacture and marketing of indigenously designed and validated agricultural equipment.

24. To use various methods, such as FM radio stations of which there are some 800 in the country, and IGNOU, for dissemination of information.

25. To ensure that the minor produce of forests is processed, to begin with by the tribals.

26. To develop, validate and market affordable precision farm machinery for small farmers that would help them add value to their products.

27. To involve creditable NGOs at every step, and to ensure that existing knowledge is used and the 'wheel not reinvented'.

Note on Radiation Sterilization of Potatoes

Radiation sterilization of potatoes can make them survive for 100-130 days at room temperature and 150-240 days at 10 degrees, depending on the variety.

Other Information

As of today, onions are exported in large quantities. There is no reason why we cannot add a hundred or more items to the existing list of such products that are exported.

Minutes of the Brainstorming Dialogue on Organic Farming Organized by Central Institute for Subtropical Horticulture and Indian Institute for Sugarcane Research (ICAR) at Lucknow on 2nd February, 2006, under the Chairmanship of Dr Mangala Rai, Director General, ICAR, and Secretary, DARE

[1] The meeting was attended by over 50 persons including farmers engaged in organic farming, commercial organisations marketing products of organic farming, the Directors and scientists of the ICAR interested and concerned with organic farming, administrators concerned with agriculture, and Dr P M Bhargava and Mrs Chandana Chakrabarti from the National Knowledge Commission.

[2] It was clear from the various presentations that ICAR has done a great deal of valuable work in the area of organic farming which needs to be more widely disseminated and shared. However, even though India is already in the field of organic farming, it needs to prepare for the future. It was repeatedly mentioned that there is going to be inevitable shift to organic agriculture around the world. At the moment, in India, the organic agriculture movement is led by farmers. Involvement of the government started in late 2004 with the conversion of the National Biofertilizer Development Centre to National Centre of Organic Farming in Ghaziabad, along with its four regional centres. Taking note of what is happening, for example in China, it was widely believed that unless we have a national policy on organic farming, a time will soon come when we would be importing organically grown food from China. Therefore, it becomes of paramount importance to have our government evolve a national policy on organic farming.

[3] The meeting brought out clearly the following highly desirable and commendable attributes of organic farming:

- It is workable and sustainable.

- It is, in the final analysis, economical for the farmers because products of organic farming command premium price. With increase in the production, premiums will level out, but the market size will increase.

- Its products are free of contamination with substances such as pesticides and heavy metal residues.

- There are less weeds to cope with when plant biomass is used as surface mulch; the weeds that grow can be used as composts/liquid manure as source for providing major and micro nutrients.

- Nitrogen applied through different composts, biofertilizers and liquid manure/vermivash to the crop at any stage of growth is sufficient and there is no need to apply nitrogen from synthetic source that pollutes atmosphere, soil and groundwater.

- It leads to improved soil health and biological properties over the years.

- It is sustainable in regard to polycrops and intercrops (example: annuals, e.g. mustard, as intercrops, with perennials, e.g. mango) as important component that are known to encourage natural enemies of crop pests, thus minimising dependence even on soft-pesticides, e.g. biopesticides.

- It often requires no or minimal inputs that the farmer needs to obtain from outside.

- It is low-cost because sufficient plant biomass as source of crop nutrients and botanicals for protecting crops can be produced by farmers, e.g. through Gliricidia, Neem, etc., grown on field bunds, and cow dung and urine. Thus shortage of farm-yard manure is not an issue.

- It does not lead to an economic backlash.

- It is saleable and feasible.

- It decreases the pest population and increases the population of parasites and predators—both in terms of quantity and diversity.

- It increases biodiversity.

[4] The difficulties with organic farming were also discussed—such as termites and rats. Those who practise organic farming have found ways and means of solving many of such problems. For example, the termitaria soil can be used as a source of nutrients and beneficial bacteria. There are, however, areas where scientists would need to focus their attention and come up with better or new solutions.

[5] It was agreed that a new institutional mechanism—perhaps a corporation or co-operative (such as a producer company, of, for and by the farmers, but manned by professionals—set up locally to cover a cluster of villages), involving farmers, the government, the ICAR and private enterprise(s), should be set up in the country. It could be one apex organisation with branches in the states at the district level and taluka, or a number of state organisations with appropriate branches. The objectives of the above-mentioned institutional mechanism should include the following:

(a) To document existing data, information, and efforts in each of the areas of organic agriculture by ICAR and others.

(b) To set up a system to collect such data on ongoing basis in real time.

(c) To collate and analyse the above data.

(d) To set up a system of disseminating useful information in the area, including the training of trainers who would eventually take the message and the methodology to the farmers.

(e) To set up a system of feedback.

(f) To interact with organisations that set up standards for organically grown food and those that certify such material.

(g) To study the market for organically grown products in India and abroad on a continuing basis.

(h) To carry out national (to meet all agri-rural and urban requirements) and international marketing.

(i) To identify research areas, and farmers to interact with the ICAR closely in this regard.

(j) To set up a system by which a farming community plans and produces its own requirements, and can get food material, besides what they grow, from the "corporation or producer company" at the farm-gate price plus a small service charge, thereby nearly doubling their purchasing power.

(k) To set up a system of sharing profits so that the farmers (in fact, all stakeholders) get an appropriate share of profit from both national and international marketing.

(l) To carry out appropriate publicity, emphasizing the advantages of organic farming.

(m) To liaison with various organizations and programmes which would help utilize the products of organic farming, such as the armed forces, employment guarantee schemes, food-for-work programmes, prisons, midday meals in schools programme, etc., which could be linked with planning of production for local supplies.

(n) To provide a single-window outlet for provision of the inputs required by farmers such as certified seeds, planting material, etc.

(o) To do what is required to have the concept of organic farming introduced in our school curricula and its technology introduced in our agriculture universities.

(p) To interact with appropriate NGOs and government missions such as the National Horticulture Mission and the Medicinal Plant Board for farmer-friendly support to organic farming schemes / proposals.

(q) To work out Standard Operating Procedures (SOPs) for organic farming under various soil and agro-climatic conditions, and to modify them from time to time in the light of new information.

[18] It was unanimously recommended that the ICAR set up an institute or national center for research and development on organic agriculture. The DG, ICAR, announced at the meeting that he would convert the Project Directorate of Cropping System Research Institute, Modipuram, one of the existing ICAR set-ups, into such an institute. This decision of the DG, ICAR, Dr Mangala Rai, was welcomed by everybody. Besides that, all concerned ICAR institutes will initiate organic farming of the mandated crops on a piece of land (declaring it as an organic field) to bring out long-term data on production and economics.

[19] It was also recommended that a group should be set up to define standards for products of *jaivik* (organic) agriculture which may be followed by farmers for domestic market labeling, as national standards for export have already been put in place by the Ministry of Commerce. The group must also work out criteria for registration of bio-pesticides and modification of international covenants to include our practices that are scientifically tenable. Again, the DG, ICAR, announced a committee consisting of Dr O P Rupela, Mr Subhash Mehta, Mr Ajay Dasgupta, Mr R A Singh, Mr Jose Samuel, and Dr T P Rajendran (ADG, ICAR) as Convenor, which would submit its report on the above within the next three months, at the time of

the next meeting in the series, which was decided to be held on energy.

[20] It was agreed that all the work on organic agriculture should be confined to what is scientifically valid or tenable.

[21] It was also agreed that while recognizing the limits of IPR, we should make full use of the IPR provisions to our advantage, e.g. by appropriately protecting our traditional (and new) practices in organic farming, and having an agricultural policy that would support organic farming and help make its products in the country the cheapest in the market.

[22] The DG, ICAR, also announced that one plot in each of the 500 Krishi Vigyan Kendras (KVKs) – one each in 500 districts of the country – will be developed as a model demonstration farm for organic farming, and that the ICAR will issue a notice to this effect immediately. Currently, only about 300 KVKs are in place. The 200-odd new KVKs may focus on the public–private partnership mentioned under (5) above. The KVKs will then demonstrate organic farming practices that meet international standards to the villagers.

[23] It was also unanimously agreed to recommend to the government to remove subsidies on fertilizers and pesticides as and where applicable. This will bring down the use of fertilizer and pesticides which have polluted country's agriculture, especially in some states of the country. The resources thus released should be used to support organic farming, e.g. by providing the infrastructure and the material it needs at a subsidized cost which would help bring down its cost to a level lower than or comparable to the cost of conventionally grown food products using synthetic fertilizers and pesticides.

[24] It was also decided that laboratories be set up in the public sector which would be internationally recognized for certification of organically grown produces. (ICAR/Ministry of Agriculture could take appropriate steps in this direction.)

[25] As of now, in many instances, sewage or compost which contains large amounts of heavy metals and pesticides, is used for production of vegetables and other crops. Given the fact that only some 25 per cent of the sewage in the country is treated, there are doors open as of now for high levels of toxic heavy metals in fruits and vegetables. A suitable law must be formulated to prevent such contamination.

February 2006

Chandana Chakrabarti

Report on the Meeting on Integrated Pest Management (IPM) and Biopesticides Organized by the ICAR as the Third Meeting in the Series Of Brainstorming Sessions on Topics Suggested by the NKC where Generation, Discussion and Use of Knowledge in the Agricultural Sector would be Important

1. The meeting was held at NAAS in New Delhi from 9.30 am to 5.00 pm on 26th April 2006.

2. The list of participants is enclosed as Annexure 4-A.

3. It was considered important that all concerned must recognize the following two facts:

   (a) Integrated pest management (IPM) does not mean "no pesticides". It minimizes the use of pesticides which could be both synthetic or natural (that would be compatible with organic farming) while maximizing protection against pests.

   (b) The world is moving slowly but surely towards organic agriculture. India, on account of its traditional knowledge repertoire, can become a leader in this movement. It would eventually mean replacement of the high dosage of pesticide used at present with pesticides that are compatible with organic farming. This would clearly need to be done in a phased manner. The first step would be the use of IPM with minimum amount of synthetic pesticides. The next step would be, through research, to replace the synthetic pesticides with pesticides and protocol that would be compatible with organic farming.

4. The present status and advantages of IPM, and problems in the use of synthetic pesticides, were extremely well documented in a paper by Amerika Singh.

The operative decisions were as follows:

(a) We should endorse the statement on IPM made in the agricultural policy of the Government of India, enunciated in 2001.

(b) The National Centre for Integrated Pest Management has already worked out methods of IPM for close to 80 crops. They should now prepare Standard Operating Procedures (SOPs) which would include formulation, data on stability and field persistence, packing and transport methodology. These SOPs should be translated into Indian languages and made available in an easy-to-use format to farmers.

(c) The ICAR should take the initiative to set up a national quality-control laboratory for material used in IPM. It should be responsible for certifying and testing IPM materials, recommending to the government the regulatory framework for their use, and working out rules for clearance by Pollution Control Boards. The above National Quality Control Laboratory or Centre may have branches in the states.

(d) A strategy for dissemination of the advantages and procedures of IPM must be worked out, for appropriate use of pesticides is vital not only to the health of our agriculture but also to human and animal health, given the fact that, often, there is an overuse of pesticides that contaminates groundwater.
   • A paragraph or two on IPM should be introduced at appropriate levels in school text-books.
   • IPM should be talked about in an organized fashion on the television and radio.
   • It should be a part of the proposed information package for Panchayats as well as a part of the activities of the proposed Village Resource Centres and the Rural Knowledge Clubs.

- In this connection, it was pointed out that while ICAR has made immense contributions to our agriculture after the Green Revolution, these contributions are not as well-known as they should be, on account of lack of an appropriate professional set-up in the ICAR for publicity and extension work. It was recommended that this lacunae in ICAR may be filled at the earliest possible, for there is no other scientific agency in the country which needs to be in as close contact with as many people as ICAR should be. It may be recalled that the Green Revolution in the 1960s in India was the consequence of superb extension work by the ICAR.

(e) An industrial set-up (perhaps, a corporation) should be put in place (either in the public sector or the private sector or the joint sector) through an initiative of the ICAR to produce all requirements, including biocontrol agents and formulations for IPM. This organization should set up a network of one-window shops for IPM around the country, perhaps, one in each taluq. The Director General of ICAR, Dr Mangala Rai, has offered to invest Rs.250 crores in such a venture out of the Rs.1178 crores of the recently approved long-term World Bank loan.

(f) An appropriate number of ITIs should be set up for training in IPM at various levels, after discussion with the ICAR. Some of them could be located within the ICAR system itself.

(g) ICAR should set up an integrated research programme on IPM-related areas. One of the objectives of this programme should be to develop IPM for crops other than those for which an IPM protocol already exists, and then to develop IPM protocols for organic farming. This could be an All-India Co-ordinated Research Project. The ICAR has agreed to set up a group to identify the areas for such research work.

"Brainstorming on IPM & Biopesticides"

List of Participants

Sl.No.	NAME
1	**Dr Mangala Rai** DG, ICAR, and Secretary, DARE, Government of India, New Delhi.
2	**Dr P M Bhargava** Vice-Chairman, National Knowledge Commission, Government of India, New Delhi.
3	**Dr Gautam Kalloo** DDG (Hort. & CS), ICAR, New Delhi.
4	**Mr Ashish Bahuguna** Joint Secretary (PP), Ministry of Agriculture, Government of India, New Delhi.
5	**Dr T P Rajendran** ADG (PP), ICAR, New Delhi.
6	**Mr Anand Shah** Deputy Secretary (PP), Ministry of Agriculture, Government of India, New Delhi
7	**Dr Amerika Singh** Director, NCIPM, ICAR, New Delhi.
8	**Dr R J Rabindra** Director, PDBC, ICAR, Bangalore.
9	**Dr (Mrs) Seema Wahab** Advisor, DBT, Government of India, New Delhi.
10	**Dr P S Chandurkar** PPA to Government of India, New Delhi.
11	**Dr N B Singh** Agricultural Commissioner, Government of India, New Delhi.
12	**Dr Upendra Koul** Director, Biopesticide Research Centre, Jalandhar.

13	**Dr B M Khadi** Director, CICR, Nagpur, Maharashtra
14	**Dr K P Jayanth** Chief Scientist, Biocontrol Research Laboratories, Bangalore (Industry representative).
15	**Sri R G Agarwal** Chairman, Crop Care Federation of India, New Delhi
16	**Dr Sandhya Kulshreshtha** Secretary, CIB
17	**Dr (Ms) Vimala Devi** Sr. Scientist (Ento.), Directorate of Rice Research, Hyderabad.
18	**Dr H S Gaur** Dean/PGS, IARI, New Delhi – 110012.
19	**Dr D V Singh** Head, Division of Plant Pathology, IARI, New Delhi – 110012.
20	**Dr G P Gupta** Head, Division of Entomology, IARI, New Delhi – 110012.
21	**Dr R P S Ahlawat** Head, Division of Agronomy, IARI, New Delhi – 110 012.
22	**Dr (Ms) Prem Dureja** Head, Division of Agrochemicals, IARI, New Delhi – 110012.
23	**Dr Pratap Singh Birthal** National Fellow, NCAP, Pusa Campus, New Delhi – 110012.
24	**Dr T P Trivedi** Principal Scientist (Entomology), NCIPM, New Delhi – 110012.
25	**Dr O M Bambawale** Principal Scientist (Pl. Path.), NCIPM, New Delhi– 110012
26	**Dr N I Yaduraju** Principal Scientist, Weed Control, IARI, New Delhi– 110012
27	**Dr P Kaur** Principal Scientist (Plant Protection Section), ICAR, New Delhi
28	**Dr D K Garg** Principal Scientist (Entomology), NCIPM, New Delhi– 110012

29	**Dr M D Jeswani** Principal Scientist (Pl. Path.), NCIPM, New Delhi– 110012
30	**Dr (Mrs) Saroj Singh** Principal Scientist (Pl. Path.), NCIPM, New Delhi.– 110012
31	**Dr A V N Paul** Principal Scientist – National Fellow (Entomology), IARI, New Delhi
32	**Dr D B Ahuja** Principal Scientist (Entomology), NCIPM, New Delhi– 110012
33	**Dr Pratibha Sharma** Principal Scientist, Plant Pathology, IARI, New Delhi
34	**Dr Chandana Chakrabarti** Hyderabad
35	**Dr O P Singh** New Delhi
36	**Mr U S Madan** Executive Director ,CCFI, New Delhi

Proceedings of the One-Day Brainstorming Session on "Energy Management in Agriculture" held at VPKAS, Almora, on 29th May, 2006

Dr H S Gupta, Director, VPKAS, Almora welcomed the Chief Guest Dr Mangala Rai, Secretary, DARE and DG, ICAR; Dr P M Bhargava, Vice-Chairman, NKC, Government of India; experts on renewable energy; and other participants **(Annexure 5-A)**.

Dr Nawab Ali, DDG (Engg.), in his introductory remarks highlighted the importance of energy and stressed the need for using renewable energy sources to meet the ever-growing energy demand on farms and also for domestic needs.

Dr P M Bhargava, Vice-Chairman, NKC, shared his views on energy research in India initiated in the late 1970s at Administrative Staff College of India, Hyderabad. He mentioned that it was during this meeting, the importance of energy plantation was realized and led to research in this new area by the Ministry of Non-Conventional Energy Sources (MNES). National Remote Sensing Agency (NRSA), Hyderabad, took up the task of mapping forest reserve areas and helping in carrying out tree plantation in areas deficient of vegetation. He said, plants are the largest user of solar energy and through photosynthesis convert it into useful products. He suggested this point needs to be advertised. He also said that our aim should be to reduce our dependence on commercial energy and replace it with renewable energy sources such as biomass, biogas, biofuel, solar, wind, farm waste utilization, etc. He emphasized the need for creating additional employment on the farm to reduce migration of rural people to urban areas.

Dr Mangala Rai, DG, ICAR, and Secretary, DARE, emphasized the need to develop clear and short-term goals and also suggest plan of action, road map and infrastructure required for use of renewable energy sources in India by keeping in mind the ground realities. He said, globally, there is an energy crisis. Hence, while suggesting alternate sources of energy for use on the farm, one needs to see its availability, utilization, cost involved and efficiency. He also said that Japan is using many times more energy than what we are using in India. He shared his experiences on energy use in drip irrigation in Israel. In Konkan region, he stressed that there is a need for plantation in the hilly areas which are at present barren.

Dr M Shyam, PC (RES), gave a brief account of recently developed renewable energy devices under the AICRP on RES. He emphasized that to promote these nine devices, large-scale demonstration needs to be carried out by MNES. He also said two designs of biogas plants have been sent to MNES for release. Dr Bhatt from MNES informed that he is pursuing the matter. **One of the recommendations that emerged from Dr Shyam's presentation was** *"To crystallize and devise a plan of action to meet the energy crisis in the rural sector of the country."* Dr Bhargava, Vice-Chairman, NKC, made the following suggestions in respect of all the nine technologies generated under the AICRP on RES.

- Economic feasibility be worked out and compared with conventional methods being used.
- Efforts be made to commercialise the technologies and suggest remedies to remove the hurdles for commercialization of the devices developed.
- Large-scale demonstration be carried out for the technologies developed.

Dr B S Pathak, Director, SPRERI, Vallab Vidyanagar, made a presentation with regard to biomass status and its scope in India. He informed the house that about 500 solar refrigerators are planned to be manufactured per year by a private industry whom SPRERI has provided the know-how. They are very useful for rural dispensaries. He emphasized the importance of decentralized power generation and use through stand-alone power plant, standby system and connectivity to grid. He gave a brief account of biomass availability in India. Taking paddy biomass as an example, he said that it could be used for installing 10 MW grid-connected power generation plant. It would require an investment of the order of Rs.60 million. About 25 hectare paddy crop would be needed to supply biomass for running this power plant. The clear point of action which emerged from Dr Pathak's presentation was that for energy scarcity areas, power generation using biomass needs to be advocated but only after proper mapping exercise is done to ensure assured supply of biomass to the plant. Dr Bhatt informed that MNES has assigned this responsibility to Indian Institute of Science at Bangalore. The following points emerged from his (Dr Pathak's) presentation:

- Establishment of biomass-based decentralized power generation plants, only after proper mapping and provision for supply of excess power to the grid.
- Preparation of a detailed project report along with economic feasibility, for decentralized power generation plants to be run by biomass, including its collection, transportation, storage, etc.
- Assessment of the availability of surplus biomass through actual collection of data rather than depending on satellite data.

Dr Ramaswamy, Dean, School of Biotechnology, SRM Institute, Kattankulathur, Tamil Nadu, emphasized the use of firewood/biomass in domestic sector to meet the rural household energy needs. It was recommended that quantity of wood used in villages and its share in the total farm energy requirement needs to be worked out. Feasibility of this technology for adoption by farmers also needs to be explored. It was also suggested that incentive to the entrepreneurs/NGOs for promoting improved and efficient *chulah*s be provided by the government and for this, immediate clear-cut action be conveyed to the concerned State agencies. Dr Bhargava suggested a mission approach for energy plantation and promotion of energy-efficient *chulah*s. For this, the nodal ministry and other organizations like TERI, MNES, Ministry of Agriculture, and Ministry of Environment & Forests may be involved.

Dr Ramaswamy also emphasized identification of more efficient bacteria/ microbes for generation of biogas from crop residues. He emphasized HRD in refinement and perfection of this technology. Use of sorghum, soyabean, molasses, wheat straw, whey, peanut hulls and other crop residues using microbes for generation of alcohol needs to be paid more attention. The following points emerged from discussion on his talk:

- Installation and promotion of improved *chulah*s and domestic biogas plants be undertaken under NREGS.
- Cost economics of use of peanut shell for gas generation needs to be worked out and its economic feasibility determined.
- A major research programme on an integrated system for complete conversion of biomass for a variety of products needs to be developed; the research component could be supported by NKC.

DG, ICAR, suggested that after every five years the data with respect to availability of wood, biomass, cow dung, etc., be collected by the centres of AICRPs on RES and other areas. He suggested that the latest data in respect of this be collected, and that this could be supported by NKC. Dr Bhargava suggested the following:

- Cost-benefit analysis for installation of biogas plants be done.
- MNES may provide an economic analysis of biogas plants based on their experience.
- Diverting of human waste to biogas plants be advertised.

Dr Dipanker De, Principal Scientist, CIAE, Bhopal, made a presentation about energy scenario in the country. He also elaborated on energy being used for raising different crops. He informed that irrigation uses 42% energy, followed by farm power (32%) and fertilizer (26%). DG, ICAR, advised him to work out the future energy demand and how it is to be met from different sources. A consensus emerged that strategies for optimum utilization of energy in farm sector need to be worked out along with different forms of energy needed to carry out different farm operations. Researchable issues need to be brought forth and an energy policy be framed for the country.

Dr B K Bhatt, Principal Scientific Officer from MNES, presented activities being carried out by his ministry. He informed that MNES is propagating the use of biogas plants and gives incentives to people who install them. He also informed that MNES has installed about 500 biogas plants for making animal feed from fish wastes. He also narrated the success story of Maharashtra where use of human waste in biogas plants for generation of biogas is being practised. **He was advised to propagate and replicate Maharashtra example in other states too.** He agreed to promote ICAR developing solid state biogas plants.

Dr H K Desai from Vidya Dairy, Anand, shared his experience with ICAR and SPRERI. Under AICRP on RES, an effluent treatment plant from cheese whey unit has been successfully installed and commercialized. It is possible to get 200 M^3 gas/day with a saving of Rs.2320 per day. He also highlighted the constraints in disposal of the effluent from the whey plants.

Mr Hitesh Shah, MD, Reliable Cattle Farm, Jabalpur, informed that he has installed four units, each of 85 m^3, of biogas plants on his farm. He further informed that he is meeting all the electrical energy need of his cattle farm from biogas obtained from his biogas plants. The digested slurry is being used as manure for crop production. He suggested that in dairy farms having large cattle population, similar biogas plants could be set up, and stations for filling the gas in cylinders may be established in villages. A mechanism needs to be developed to market organic manure obtained from biogas plants. He stressed the need for establishment of a fodder bank, promotion of balers and storage of fodder. Dr Bhargava suggested that Mr Shah could take a lead in promoting biogas plants for generation of electricity. He was asked to suggest a model and strategies to implement the model. Possibility of starting a Revolving Fund Scheme (RFS) needs to be explored for an individual or an organization constructing the biogas plants, using carbon credit funds. India should install biogas plants for generation of electricity and claim carbon credit funds.

Mr Narendra Yardi, MD, NRC Tech, a manufacturer of solar gadgets, informed that he is making solar dryers; the payback period is 3 years. **He was advised to work out the economics of solar drying.**

Dr B C Jain, MD, Ankur Scientific, a manufacturer of renewable energy gadget and biomass-based gasifier power plants producer, shared his experience in this area. He emphasized the use of biomass for generation of power. Dr Bhargava advised him to provide the relative cost economics of power generation by biomass and ordinary fuel. He suggested the following:
- Upgrade fuel quality obtained from biomass gasifier.
- Run pumps on biofuels.
- Improve tail-end grid quality.
- Use biomass for power generation.

Mr Munesh Goyal, Retired IAS & Chief Secretary, Vidya Bhawan, Udaipur, said that more extension work is needed to promote use of efficient renewable energy gadgets. Government of India should give more incentive to people/industry using renewable energy sources. Hence, a consensus emerged that more effective extension activity and demonstration of RES-based gadgets and plants be undertaken under the aegis of NKC by AICRP or RES/state governments.

Dr Arun Kumar from Product Development Alternatives, an NGO from New Delhi, shared his experience in promotion of renewable energy, especially in North Bihar. He narrated his experience of installing 12 energy-efficient pumps which helped the villagers to obtain a second crop. They promoted growing of energy-intensive crops, which fetched the farmer an additional income of Rs.500 per tonne. **He suggested providing some incubation funds for taking up these type of activities by NGOs/entrepreneurs.**

Mr S S Rao from NRC for Sorghum, Hyderabad, informed that they have perfected the technology for ethanol production from sorghum. It was recommended that the use of ethanol from sorghum needs to be promoted at the country level. He also expressed the need for development of a machine for crushing of sorghum and a sorghum harvester for cutting the crop. **R&D on use of sorghum and sugarcane-based ethanol for mixing with diesel should be pursued and demonstration plants, under NKC, be set up.**

Dr G Kalloo, DDG (Crop & Horticulture), ICAR, suggested integration of various sources of energy for more efficient utilization on the farm. Before advocating such a technology, its technological feasibility and socio-economic benefit need to be worked out.

Presentations made by experts and the experiences narrated by the representatives of some of the NGOs, SHGs and government organisations on the use of renewable energy at farms for various operations were discussed thoroughly, from which the following **nine recommendations emerged**.

1. The nine new energy saving technologies developed by the All India Coordinated Research Project on Renewable Energy Sources, including a new design of a bio-gas plant that requires very

little water, should be promoted through appropriate extension mechanisms so that it reaches the users.

(Action: Project Coordinator, AICRP, on Renewable Energy Sources)

2. The national energy policy should include energy generation from surplus biomass/crop residue. A consortium of organizations such as MNES, ICAR, Department of Agriculture of Delhi and National Remote Sensing Agency (NRSA) should work out technologies for using the surplus biomass residue. The consortium should also work out the economics of the technologies developed and a mechanism of dissemination and marketing of technologies which may be different for different regions and different kinds of biomass. For this purpose, the Government of India should set up an appropriate mission which would determine the amount of surplus biomass residue available in the country, have the technologies for the use of the biomass developed, the economics of the technologies assessed, and mechanism of their dissemination and marketing worked out.

(Action: NKC / ICAR / MNES)

3. The importance of the continued use of biomass, such as firewood as a source of energy in the rural areas, must be recognized and mechanisms for increasing the efficiency and convenience of such use (such as smokeless *chulhas*) worked out. The marketing of such efficiency and convenience enhancing technologies to the people must be taken as a major extension project by the ICAR / Department of Agriculture, Government of India.

(Action: PC, RES)

4. A well thought out programme of "energy plantations" should be worked out and implemented. The country may need as many as 300,000 such plantations in the rural sector. The NRSA may identify the sites for such plantations – an exercise which, indeed, may already have been done. The plants suitable for

such plantations in the various regions of the country should be identified, and enough seeds / plantation material made available to sustain the plantations. Each village or group of villages should have three areas earmarked for such plantations of trees / plants that will grow firewood in the required quantities. The Ministry of Agriculture may be appointed the nodal agency for this purpose. Such plantations would go a long way in relieving the drudgery of the village housewives who spend considerable proportion of their working hours in collecting firewood. Each of the three plantations could be harvested over three successive years and replanted after harvesting. The village panchayat could set up a system for harvesting the plantations to provide the required amount of firewood, and delivering it to the households in the village / villages.

(Action: NKC / ICAR / Ministries of Rural Development, Panchayati Raj, and Environment & Forests)

5. Several research areas relevant to either increasing the availability of energy or reducing the use of energy in agriculture were mentioned. For example, a small increase in the efficiency of photosynthesis could make a dramatic change in the biomass availability for generation of energy. Conversion of rice from a C-3 to C-4 crop could revolutionize the process of growing rice. Similarly, the need for developing an integrated system for complete conversion of biomass to a variety of products was very well articulated. For example, an integrated process for the use of peanut hull has been developed. Eventually, we should be able to have a process for conversion of cellulose to glucose and then to alcohol. It was mentioned that a new, genetically engineered cellulase (the enzyme that breaks cellulose) has been developed, which does not have the disadvantages of native cellulase. The ICAR should also take up the development of an artificial rumen, the extra organ which humans don't have but which allows cattle to digest cellulase.

(Action: ICAR / PC, RES)

6. It was recommended that agriculture should be put on the concurrent list. It was also strongly felt that animal husbandry, fisheries, agriculture, fertilizers and other agrochemicals must all be dealt with by a single department—the Department of Agriculture / ICAR. As of today, they are dealt with by different departments of GOI, which does not allow taking an integrated approach towards development of activities that today come under the purview of these segmented departments. The need for ICAR being actively and intimately involved in extension work was emphasized all through the meeting. It was estimated that ICAR would need at least 5000 additional extension workers for it to optimally utilize its own capabilities and outcome of research.

(Action: NKC)

7. It was suggested that a revolving fund for entrepreneurs who set up a community biogas plant should be instituted. Such plants should give a return of 16-20 percent. The entrepreneur should be a Panchayat or an energy cooperative set up by a group of villages or entrepreneurs. The fund should act like an incubator, with the money that is provided to entrepreneurs designated to be returned within a reasonable period with a low rate of interest. It could operate on the basis of something like the technology development fund of the Department of Science & Technology. The corpus of this fund, eventually, should be Rs.1,000 crores.

(Action: NKC / MNES / ICAR)

The meeting ended with a vote of thanks to the chair and other participants including the host VPKAS, Almora, by Dr S K Tandon, ADG (Engineering), ICAR , New Delhi.

List of Participants for the Brainstorming Session on
"Energy Management in Agriculture"
held at VPKAS, Almora, on 29th May, 2006

ICAR
1. **Dr Mangala Rao**, Secretary, DARE & DG, ICAR, New Delhi
2. **Dr Nawab Ali**, DDG (Engg.), ICAR, Pusa, KAB-II, New Delhi
3. **Dr G Kalloo**, DDG (Hort.), ICAR, Pusa, KAB-II, New Delhi
4. **Dr H S Gupta**, Director, VPKAS, Almora
5. **Dr M M Pandey**, Director, CIAE, Bhopal
6. **Dr S K Tandon**, ADG (Engg.), CIAE, Bhopal
7. **Dr D De**, Principal Scientist, CIAE, Bhopal
8. **Dr S S Rao**, Principal Scientist, National Research Centre for Sorghum, Hyderabad

Other than ICAR
9. **Dr P M Bhargava**, Vice-Chairman, National Knowledge Commission, Government of India, New Delhi
10. **Ms Chandana Chakrabarti**, National Knowledge Commission, c/o Centre for Policy Research, Dharma Marg, Chanakyapuri, New Delhi–110 021
11. **Dr T K Bhattacharya**, Senior Research Engineer & ADR (Engg.), Department of Farm Power & Machinery Engineering, GBPUA&T, Pantnagar-263 145

Experts
12. **Dr B S Pathak,** Director, SPREPI, Post bag No.2, Vallabh Vidyanagar-380 120 (Gujarat)
13. **Dr B K Bhatt**, Principal Scientific Officer, Ministry of Non-Conventional Energy Sources, Block No. 14, CGO Complex, Lodhi Road, New Delhi-110 003

14. **Mr Arun Kumar**, President, Development Alternatives, 111/g-Z, Kishangarh, Vasant Kunj, New Delhi-110 070
15. **Dr B C Jain,** Managing Director, M/s. Ankur Scientific Energy Technologies Pvt. Ltd., Ankur, Near Old Sama Jakat Naka, Vadodara-390 008 (Gujarat)
16. **Mr Munesh Goyal,** IAS (Rtd.), Former Chief Secretary, Vidya Bhawan Society, 805, Hiran Magri, Sector-4, Nr. Jain Mandir, Udaipur-313 003 (Rajasthan)
17. **Mr Hitesh Shah**, Director, Reliable Cattle Farm, 1621, Napier Town, Jabalpur 482 001 (Madhya Pradesh)
18. **Mr H K Desai**, Managing Director, Vidya Dairy, Anand Agricultural University Campus, Anand–380 110 (Gujarat)
19. **Dr K Ramaswamy**, Dean, School of Biotechnology, SRM Institute (Deemed University), Kattaankulathur-603 203 (Tamil Nadu)
20. **Mr N R Yardi**, MD, M/s. NRG Technologies Pvt. Ltd., 989/6, GIDC Estate, Makarpura, Vadodara–390 010 (Gujarat)

MSS/DB
27 November 2006

Dr P M Bhargava
Bhargava.pm@gmail.com

My dear Pushpa,

It was a pleasure meeting you, Jayati Ghosh and Chandana on 19th November. I greatly benefited from our discussion. I have gone through carefully the papers you gave me. The research needs of farmers which have been identified are all very important. In particular I am happy that you have done detailed work on post-harvest technology, organic farming, traditional knowledge, integrated pest-management and information and knowledge flow to rural sector. All these issues have also been discussed in detail in the five reports of the National Commission on Farmers and in the Draft National Policy for Farmers. Your support and additional suggestions would be very helpful in the development of priorities for the eleventh plan period. I therefore express my sincere gratitude to you for mobilizing the analytical strength and the intellectual capability of the Knowledge Commission for helping our rural families. In case there is any particular issue on which you would like my comment, I shall always be happy to share my experience.

I wish you and Chandana great success in the very important work you both are doing.

With affectionate regards,

Yours affly,

M S Swaminathan

PROF M S SWAMINATHAN
President, Pugwash Conferences on Science and World Affairs
Chairman, M S Swaminathan Research Foundation
Third Cross Street, Taramani Institutional Area
Chennai – 600 113 (India)
Tel: +91 44 2254 2790 / 2254 1229; Fax: +91 44 2254 1319
Email: swami@mssrf.res.in / msswami@vsnl.net

MSS/DB/
3 December 2006

Dr. P M Bhargava
Vice Chairman, National Knowledge Commission
Government of India, Hyderabad
Bhargava.pm@gmail.com
Pmb1928@yahoo.co.in

My dear Pushpa,

Thank you very much for your kind letter. I am coming to Hyderabad tomorrow evening and hence I shall bring a copy of the final report of NCF personally. I will be staying at Taj Krishna and have to attend the meeting in the Administrative Staff College on 5th morning.

You should certainly send the reports you gave me to the Prime Minister. They are all very important and supplement very well the recommendations of NCF. I am grateful to you for all that you are doing to accelerate the progress of sustainable agriculture in our country.

I fully agree with you that we should have an effective Hazard Analysis Critical Control Point and GMP in our animal feed sector. NCF has also recommended regional centres for Food Security and Safety for this purpose. We should not lose further time in implementing your suggestion.

With warm personal regards,

Yours affly,

M S Swaminathan

Encl: a/a
PS: Enclosure : Prof M S Swaminathan will hand over to you personally

PROF M S SWMINATHAN
President, Pugwash Conferences on Science and World Affairs
Chairman, M S Swaminathan Research Foundation
Third Cross Street, Taramani Institutional Area
Chennai – 600 113 (India)
Tel: +91 44 2254 2790 / 2254 1229; Fax: +91 44 2254 1319
Email: swami@mssrf.res.in / msswami@vsnl.net

MSS/DB
4 April 2007

Dr. Pushpa M Bhargava
Bhargava.pm@gmail.com
Pmb1928@yahoo.co.in

My dear Pushpa,

Thank you very much for your kind letter. I am most grateful for your generous sentiments. I also look forward to spending a few hours with you discussing issues of common concern. I am only sorry that your visionary ideas which you explained to me when we had dinner along with Dr Jayati Ghosh are not receiving the attention and action they so richly deserve.

With warm personal regards,

Yours sincerely,

M S Swaminathan

PROF M S SWMINATHAN
President, Pugwash Conferences on Science and World Affairs
Chairman, M S Swaminathan Research Foundation
Third Cross Street, Taramani Institutional Area
Chennai – 600 113 (India)
Tel: +91 44 2254 2790 / 2254 1229; Fax: +91 44 2254 1319
Email: swami@mssrf.res.in / msswami@vsnl.net

Appendix 8

The titles/salient features of randomly selected newspaper reports on wastage of grain in India on account of inadequate storage facility.

The Hindu: Hindu
The New Indian Express: NIE
The Times of India: TOI
Deccan Chronicle: DC
Deccan Herald: DH

(only titles and sub-titles are given in most cases)

(1)   DC. September 12, 2010
      Why are 350m Indians hungry? India is the second fastest
      growing economy in the world. If you heard this somewhere in
      sub-Saharan Africa, you would think everyone in India must be
      well-fed, what with the country's food grain surplus. But, by the
      government's own admission, some 350 million Indians go hungry
      every day. Worse, in a country where every middle-class parent
      teaches her child not to waste even a morsel of food on the plate,
      the government lets millions of tonnes of food grains rot. The
      PM says policy on what to do with all that food grain is his realm,
      not the Supreme Court's. But the nation wonders: has food and
      agriculture become a blindspot for his government?

(2)   DC. October 28, 2010
      Storage woes for bumper crop. While a bumper paddy crop
      should cheer the farmers in the State, lack of adequate storage
      and transport facilities is leaving them worried.

(3)   Hindu. October 28, 2011
      Lack of storage hits farm sector. 'India losing Rs.40,000 crore in
      wastage of farm produce'.

(4)   TOI. April 4, 2012
      Bumper crop growth leads to catch-22 situation.

(5) DC. May 11, 2012
Grain of truth. Labourers sort through sacks of rotting grains while trying to salvage any that is still edible at an open storage area in Khamanon village, 215 km from Amritsar. Millions of tonnes of wheat are rotting in the open due to shortage of warehouse space to store the growing grain stockpiles. Food minister KV Thomas said on Thursday that the government is taking "all necessary steps" to increase the storage capacities. He said the government is also looking at private partnerships to attract investment in building warehouses and new storage spaces would be available by the end of the year.

(6) DH. May 17, 2012
'A national grid of grain storages needed to prevent wastage'.

(7) NIE. May 11, 2012
Food for thought. A labourer pulling a sack of rotten wheat in a bid to salvage edible grains at an open storage area in Khamonan village near Amritsar.

(8) TOI. May 15, 2012
No storage space for bumper harvest, warns food ministry. FCI earlier had issued alarm on the issue.

(9) NIE. September 10, 2012
Rats eat away paddy worth Rs.325 crore in EG district. Rat poison worth lakhs of rupees has not been used properly.

(10) TOI. October 1, 2012
No storage space for bumper stock in govt godowns. Haryana, Punjab mandis packed with previous year's produce.

(11)   DC. October 17, 2012
       1.3b tonne of grain lost yearly. Natural farming methods must for
       future food security.

(12)   DC. September 12, 2012
       Food on global casino. Putting food on global casino is serving
       speculative investors, not people. We need to get food back on
       people's plates.

(13)   TOI. January 19, 2013
       Rains damage grains in Punjab, Haryana.

Appendix 9

"Our Expectations from the Police", Pushpa M Bhargava,
The Tribune, 14th June, 2008

Consider the following cases: Binayak Sen held for a year in a jail in Chhattisgarh without trial and without a shred of hard evidence against him. The numerous other atrocities committed by police-supported Salwa Judum in Chhattisgarh ...

The Anti-Terrorism Squad and the Special Task Force of UP police picking up, detaining and interrogating suspected terrorists in flagrantly illegal ways, with no lawyer agreeing to take up their case because they are all Muslims ...

"Encounter" deaths of innocent people caused by the police under the garb of fighting left-wing extremism ...

Rapes and murders galore by members of the police force that is actually paid to prevent rape and murder ...

And innumerable acts of omission such as not accepting FIRs, if inconvenient.

If we could have Lodhas of Bengal considered as a criminal tribe, it would be surely justified for the Indian Council of Social Science Research (ICSSR), in view of the above, to fund a study to determine if the tribe of the police should be done the same honour.

That leads us to the question: what may we judge our police by? I dare say we may do so against the following ten expectations of civil society from the police:

Professionalism: Just look at the way traffic police operates in say, Hyderabad. They have no idea of what the rules of the road are: not even what a one-way street means.

Honesty and integrity: Today, those who don't have a price in the police are unlikely to last for long.

Respect for human rights: The police station is, for civil society, one of the most dreaded places to go to. It has become virtually synonymous with torture, insult, rape, and apathy to basic human rights.

Courtesy: Have you ever heard a policeman say sorry or thank you?

Help: Can you recall the last time a policeman was helpful to you, say at the police station, if you went there with a genuine complaint and are neither rich nor famous nor know somebody who is rich or famous or powerful?

A minimal understanding of basic human needs and human behaviour: If they had that understanding they wouldn't think that the only solution to left-wing extremism is through the gun.

Ability to resist political pressure in the discharge of duties: If this were so, the brats of the rich and the powerful would not be able to break all traffic rules with such impunity,

Commitment to the country, to its objectives, and to its values: What we see, instead, in our law enforcement set-up, is a total commitment to oneself and surrender to political, bureaucratic and money power, Police and sycophancy have become a lethal combination for the civil society in our country.

Strict law enforcement (and, therefore, awareness of law!): Otherwise, how would the maximum number of traffic violations and violation of building norms occur right under the nose of the police?

Being proactive: The road contractors, at least in my city of Hyderabad—specially in areas where the rich, the powerful and the famous don't live—after doing whatever job they were supposed to do (no matter how badly), leave all the waste material by the road side which the police sees day in and day out. Have they ever made a complaint against the contractors and the builders having behaved so irresponsibly?

In a fair marking system, with ten marks for each of the above ten expectations, I dare say 1 per cent of our police force will probably receive over 90 per cent; 4 per cent between 75 and 90; 5 per cent between 60 and 75, 45 and 60, and 30 and 45 each; and 75 per cent below 30 marks. So there is much space for improvement!

I believe there is a police bill on the anvil for consideration by the Parliament. But, perhaps, it is too much to expect that the law makers will not behave like the police itself and take note of the above expectations of the civil society from the police.

It is unfortunate that it is not understood that such a situation, where keepers of law become breakers of law, and makers of law become insensitive to the miseries and problems of people, cannot last for long. Remember the French Revolution. We may well be headed for a similar one.

Appendix 10

What Sri Lanka did with its jackfruit: A lesson for India.

How Sri Lanka grew a thriving agro-industry

JACKFRUIT BUSINESS
Shree Padre, Colombo
(Reproduced from *Civil Society*, July 2012)

Anula Sirisena is a Sri Lankan housewife from a poor family. She lives in a village near Kandy. Anula has seven jackfruit trees on her piece of land. But her jackfruits used to go waste since she didn't know how to earn money from trees.

About seven years ago Anula's life changed for the better. She enrolled at the Horticulture Crop Research and Development Institute (HORDI) run by the Sri Lankan government's Ministry of Agriculture. HORDI taught her to make *sambal*, chutney and pickle from tender jackfruit, called *polos* in Sinhala. All three are staple additives in Sinhalese meals.

Anula now runs a microenterprise in jackfruit products under the Samanala brand name. 'Samanala' means butterfly. Her husband Sirisena, helps her or she hires an extra hand, if needed. Her neatly packaged and labeled products are retailed at the Ministry of Agriculture's sales centre in Peradeniya. Anula produces a few other processed foodstuffs too. Her family now earns 50,000 Sri Lankan rupees a year.

Historically the jackfruit has always enjoyed the status of a holy tree in Sri Lanka. Named *baat gasa* or 'rice tree', it is said to have saved Lankans from hunger in a crisis. Jackfruit has social and religious connotations too in Sri Lanka. In recent years it is the economic significance of jackfruit that has grown. Since the past 10 years HORDI, funded by the International Centre for Underutilized Crops (ICUC), has trained street vendors, housewives and entrepreneurs free of cost in minimal processing, dehydration, and bottling technologies. The institute's ex-students now manufacture a range of jackfruit products for the domestic and export market. So the jackfruit not only staves hunger, it yields jobs and money.

It isn't HORDI alone that is training people. Around 14 institutions have pitched in. NGOs and others charge a fee. The Industrial Training Institute (ITI) has in the last 20 years organized 200 workshops and trained 2,000 people in minimal processing of jackfruit.

As a result Sri Lanka has become the world leader in making jackfruit the key to food security and raising the incomes of the poor. Short duration training and support have empowered rural families. Each household has a few jackfruit trees that the family can't wholly consume. They now know how to convert their jackfruits into products for sale in urban markets.

Most jackfruit enterprises on the island are not high-end companies but medium scale operators and home industries. This strategy has made jackfruit products affordable for everyone.

According to Dr Subha Heenkenda, Research Officer at HORDI, the total area under jackfruit on the island is 50,000 hectares. "So our country will never starve," says Dr Subha proudly. On an average, each tree bears 35 fruits of 20 kg each. According to HORDI's estimates, the island's total annual production of jackfruit is 1400,000 tonnes.

STREETS AND MARKETS: "Minimal processing is the easiest business to start," says Senarath Ekanayake, Research Officer, Food Research Unit in HORDI, the key person behind training in jackfruit value addition and minimal processing. "You don't need any heavy investment or machinery. You can start at 3 am, pack your products by 6 am and send your consignment off in the first bus. You don't make any losses even if you don't produce anything for a day or two. Unlike pickle, jam or jelly, you don't have to wait for months."

Take Manel Sriyani, who trained at HORDI. Manel and her family have been producing four varieties of ready-to cook products from tender jackfruit *(polos)* and unripe jackfruit *(kos)*. They sell around 120 packets per day. A 250gm pack is priced at Rs.25/-. Her packets sell in local shops and at the agriculture department's sales counter. She also supplies to three supermarkets in Kandy.

"We are happy because this is a business we can manage ourselves with occasional help from outside," says Manel Sriyani. "One of our requirements is a machine to chop the peeled tender jackfruits. This part of our work requires three hours and a lot of energy." Their small old house is now being remodeled to earn, thanks to minimal processing of jackfruit.

Sri Lanka has around 70 units today which produce ready-to-cook jackfruit after minimal processing. These packets are sold to vegetable shops and supermarkets. Then, there are hundreds of street vendors who cut jackfruit in front of their customers or sell pre-packed jackfruit. "Vissa, vissa!", you hear vendors shouting in Kandy's busy market. 'Vissa' means 'cheap' and it is freshly cut jackfruit that is on offer.

The jackfruit is cut into three different shapes for three different curries. The cube shape—exclusively meant for *polos* curry—is the most popular. For *polos mellum*, tender jackfruit is chopped into small bits. Very few vendors sell jackfruit in large pieces for making cutlets or dunking into biryani.

Antony, 47, who sells freshly cut jackfruit on a cart in Colombo's Malay Street says it is his family business. He joined his father about 35 years ago. Antony's team of four begins cutting jackfruit at 5 am. They sell till noon. A kilo of freshly cut jackfruit is priced at Rs.60. On an average they sell around a quintal. Antony also sells *waraka,* a fruity jackfruit and *tambili,* a large coconut variety for which Sri Lanka is famous. He closes business at noon and begins once again at 3 pm continuing till sunset.

DRIED JACKFRUIT: Sri Lanka has also been very successful in training poorer communities in dehydration, a technology that extends the shelf life of vegetables and fruits up to six months at least. Menike Wijekoon from Rajawell is a recent entrant into the jackfruit value addition business. She used to work at a dolomite factory. Menike decided to switch careers and enrolled for a four-day training programme on dehydration of fruits and vegetables at the Vidhatha Centre run by Sri Lanka's Ministry of Technology.

After training she invested in a 25 kg capacity drier. Today, her flagship product is dehydrated unripe jackfruit. She also produces dehydrated bitter gourd, brinjal, curry leaves, kohila and ladyfingers. Neatly packed under her brand name, Pradeepa. Menika's products are also sold at the Peradeniya Sales Centre.

A 200 gm packet of dehydrated unripe jackfruit is priced at Rs.145. This jackfruit can be used to make curry after soaking the dried chunks in water for 30 minutes. But since fresh vegetables are available at a cheaper price, Menike's clientele consists mainly of non-resident Sri Lankans who pick up her products to take them back to the country they work in, so Menike could say her business is mainly export-oriented.

One of her interesting products is jack seed powder, globally recognized as a very nutritious food. Sri Lankans use it to make a crispy snack called *murukku*. A 200 gm packet of Menike's jack seed powder costs Rs.60. Although sales are not that brisk, Menike says she manages to sell about 50 kg a year of jack seed powder.

The leader in popularizing dehydration technology is the Rural Enterprises Network (REN) started in 2002. REN emerged from a micro-enterprise project of Practical Action, a poverty eradication programme started by the Intermediate Technology Development Group. REN develops micro and small-scale rural enterprises by helping them with a range of business development services. It promotes processed agro-produce under a common brand name, nationally and in global markets.

REN is a pioneer in unripe jackfruit dehydration. Practical Action did a lot of R&D with different types of driers. They have developed low-cost driers that run on firewood and sawdust. Electric driers are very expensive. "Jackfruit is one of our products," clarifies Nilantha Athapattu, a manager with REN. "We have large production units with 200 kg capacity driers and 45 small-scale driers that can dry 20 kg in a batch. Jackfruit dehydration goes on for about eight months."

People are trained in batches. Each unit consists of five or eight people. Another two or three trainees are responsible for raw material collection. In fact, ordinary village women now produce dehydrated jackfruit and other products at quality acceptable to supermarkets. This is an enviable achievement for REN.

According to Nilantha, each unit procures jackfruit from around 50 households. This means REN must be helping more than 1,500 families earn more from their jackfruit. "There are families who earn between Rs.3,000 and Rs.4,000 rupees a month," says Nilantha.

Since the last three years, REN has diversified into bottling jackfruit products. There is a training course. Five groups are manufacturing on an average 1,000 bottles per month of *polos* curry, *kos* in brine, tender jackfruit in brine, *polos mellum* and *polos sambal.*

Unlike REN, Vista Natural Products in Aranayake near Kandy is trying to sell its dehydrated unripe jackfruit in local markets. This three-year-old unit run by Dr. Jagath Elvitigala produces three types of dehydrated jackfruit to match three kinds of *kos* curries—Kiri Kos, Kos Thambuma and Kos Melluma.

Dr. Elvitigala's unit employs four women and works for three days a week. Freshly peeled jackfruit bulbs are bought, thus avoiding the bother of employing labour to do this at the unit. "Marketing is our biggest bottleneck," says B.M. Ariyarathna, who is the unit's manager. "In supermarkets they ask us for discounts up to 30 per cent and demand extended credit. We are selling to a few restaurants too."

But the adventurous doctor, who has settled in this village from Colombo, is not ready to give up. He has planted selected grafts of jackfruit on five acres. These trees have now started to yield fruits. "I want to set up the industry here. This way we can achieve quality with our own raw material and hopefully improve our market base."

LOCAL TO GLOBAL: The big companies have not lagged behind. Sri Lanka has about 10 to 12 big companies who have been producing and marketing jackfruit products for over a decade. These are exported to 10 to 15 countries. Their customers are Sri Lankans living and working abroad.

There is no domestic demand for canned or bottled jackfruit products even in local supermarkets. Fresh jackfruit is available at a lower price in local markets.

"When we started our first factory in 1989, we gave priority to jackfruit products. At that time there was huge demand from Asians living abroad," says Nimal Jayasuriya, managing director of Foreconns Canneries.

But now, he says, the industry is facing two major challenges. "Bottles and tins are very expensive here since they have to be mainly imported. Thai companies are giving us stiff competition in products like tender jackfruit in brine since labour is cheaper there. We are able to retain our market only in our traditional products like *polos* curry and *polos mellum*," says Nimal.

Australia has emerged as a major market for Araliya Exports based in Colombo. "When we started a decade ago, only one or two companies were making jackfruit products. Today that number has increased to more than 10," says Mailvaganam Rajkumar, managing director of Araliya Exports. "Jackfruit products are very easy to produce and convenient for Western consumers. You just need to heat and eat."

Araliya's jackfruit products are exported to Canada, the US, Switzerland and Male Island. Every year exports increase by five to 10 per cent. Their most recent importer is China which is buying *polos* curry. There is good scope for market expansion. But what is lacking is awareness of the nutritional value of jackfruit in the West.

Interestingly, *polos* curry is so popular in Sri Lanka that it almost seems to be a national dish. Everybody from roadside restaurants to five star hotels serves it. Explains an elderly Sri Lankan gentleman. "You place *polos* curry on the table with other non-vegetarian curries. Your guests will first have *polos* curry and then the fish or chicken curries."

Another curry gaining popularity in Australia is Kallu Pol Maluwa. This dish is made with jack seed powder and fried coconut. Like *polos* curry, it is a traditional Sri Lankan recipe.

It is generally agreed that the commercial *polos* curries don't match up to the traditionally made dish. "The taste of the traditional curry made in a few villages is much better. It takes two entire days to prepare *polos* curry. And it has to be cooked in an earthen pot on a low flame," says Senarath Ekanayake.

THEN AND NOW: Sri Lanka's jackfruit journey has come a long way since freshly cut jackfruit was first introduced on streets and in markets after 1977, when the economy began to liberalise. Now, according to Wasantha

Wijewardhane, a social activist, "Jackfruit attracts more urban consumers because it is very safe unlike other pesticide-ridden vegetables. It is slowly attaining the status of a money-spinning crop. It is not uncommon for a jackfruit weighing a kg to sell for Rs.100 in Colombo. Many people now want to plant jackfruit."

Twenty five years ago the jackfruit scenario was bleak here. Lorry loads of jackfruit brought from Ratnapura or Badulla were offloaded cheap in the markets of Colombo.

Now farmers have realized that jackfruit fetches money. If one jackfruit is sold in Colombo for Rs.100, the farmer probably makes only Rs.10. But it is still bringing in an income so cutting of jackfruit trees has decreased.

However, training people in minimal processing, dehydration and bottling technologies has yet to reach far-flung villages, says Padma Pushpakanthi, national secretary of Savisthri, a women's NGO working for jackfruit development. She says in her village, Walapola in Kegalle district, jackfruit which is not consumed by the family just goes waste. These simple technologies of drying or minimal processing have not reached my village, she says.

According to Dr Heenkenda, Sri Lanka consumes about 25 to 30 per cent of its tender jackfruit as a vegetable. The minimal processing enterprises —both trained and untrained vendors—have increased the consumption of jackfruit by 10 per cent. This is not a small achievement. "But all said and done," he says, "our total consumption will not surpass a paltry 25 per cent." Wasantha Wijewardane, on the other hand, says probably around 50 per cent of Sri Lanka's jackfruit is consumed domestically.

Another drawback is that jackfruit is not popular as a fruit. Efforts to do so have been relegated to the backseat. With its considerable inflow of tourists and mushrooming supermarkets, Sri Lanka could make fresh bulb sales popular. Sweets like jackfruit *varatty*, which Kerala is famous for, or jackfruit *papad* and sweet *papad* are unknown in Sri Lanka. Preservation of jackfruit in sugar syrup is somewhat popular.

It is also surprising that Sri Lanka's processed jackfruit products have not made any inroads into the Indian market. Both in south and north India, Sri Lanka's *polos* curry, tender jack in brine, jack seed curry etc. would attract buyers.

Today tender jackfruit and ripe jackfruit are available in Colombo throughout the year. The minimal processing units produce ready-to-cook tender jackfruit for 10 months. They take a two-month gap not because raw material is not available but because it turns out to be expensive.

"There used to be two jackfruit seasons here," says Sarananda Hewage, a senior horticulture officer. "The *yala* season from March to August and the *maha* season from November to January. But now we get jackfruit through the year in Colombo," says Hewage.

Sunil, a roadside vendor on the Kandy-Colombo highway, doesn't close his shop unless he has some emergency to attend to. He always stocks mature jackfruit, which he personally selects and sources from nearby villages. Perhaps it is time the seasonal tag was removed from jackfruit.

We, in India, can learn a lot from Sri Lanka's experience in using natural resources and doing value addition. It is a tribute to the Sri Lankan spirit that despite internal conflict and turmoil, the island has forged ahead. It has achieved success in the production and marketing of treacle and jaggery, curries from breadfruit and banana flower, jam from wood apple, herbal tea and many other processed products. This is indicative of their enterprising nature and hard work.

Appendix 11

A letter to the Prime Minister regarding what India should do to optimally utilize its traditional knowledge.

May 8, 2007

Dr Manmohan Singh
Prime Minister of India
7, Race Course Road
New Delhi 110011

My dear Prime Minister,

Today, the world over, both in developed and developing countries, there is an increasing emphasis on traditional knowledge and its use to create products and services of value, in addition to providing employment and generating wealth. Most countries have set up organizations to encourage this effort, so much so that the term "creative and cultural industries" based on traditional knowledge and skills has now become a part of our common vocabulary.

India has, perhaps, the longest tradition in this regard and a variety that is unparalleled. We have, however, not used even a small fraction of our potential in the area of traditional knowledge, not only to generate wealth and provide employment but also to raise the prestige of our country in the international arena. In fact, traditional knowledge has in our country the potential to generate employment for at least one hundred million people and generate an income of Rs.600,000 crores a year.

When I was a member of the National Knowledge Commission (NKC) and had taken the responsibility of looking at traditional knowledge, we identified the following areas of traditional knowledge for active pursuit:

(1) Traditional medical and healthcare systems that are not incompatible with science, with special reference to plant-based drugs and yoga.
(2) Traditional agricultural practices.
(3) Optimum utilization of our vegetables and fruits.

(4) Leveraging traditional practices for tourism.

(5) Leveraging our creative, cultural and legacy traditions for employment and wealth generation.

(6) Water harvesting using traditional practices.

After extensive discussion with stakeholders, we finalized our recommendations in the first five of the above areas. These finalized recommendations were sent a couple of months ago to the Chairman of the NKC, but I do not believe any action has been taken or is likely to be taken by the NKC on these recommendations, as traditional knowledge has not been important for the NKC. This will be clear from the fact that even though I held the first meeting on traditional knowledge on behalf of the NKC in December 2005 (one-and-a-half years ago), and the minutes of these meetings and the decision taken at it were communicated to the members of NKC immediately afterwards, no note was taken of it by the NKC in spite of my repeated reminders. Ruefully, I turned out to be the only member of the NKC who felt that traditional knowledge, which has been an integral part of our heritage, was valuable and should be encouraged/pursued and ethically exploited for improvement of the economic and social life of those who practiced it and who were largely located in the rural sector. The optimal utilization of traditional knowledge is thus bound to play an important role in the development of our rural sector. I am, therefore, enclosing our recommendations on Traditional Knowledge (Annexure 1).

The salient points of these recommendations are as follows:

(i) A national mission on plant-based drug formulations, yoga and other traditional medical and health practices that are compatible with science should be set up, with a sub-mission for each of the above-mentioned three areas. Such an effort will allow us, for example, to ethically commercialise the standardized and validated plant–based drug formulations out of the 40,000 or so we have in our traditional systems of medicine.

(ii) We have over 4,000 traditional agricultural practices that have been documented, out of which over 90 have been validated and nearly 40 cross validated till December 2005. An appropriate mission should be set up for validation and commercialisation of all these practices. The mission should involve the National Innovation Foundation and the Indian Council of Agricultural Research; it could become a model of cooperation between Government and the civil society in an area which is of the utmost importance to the country.

(iii) We have some 150 documented vegetables and, perhaps, an equal number of fruits, on which a great deal of nutritional and other scientific information is available; many of them have been shown to have remarkable pharmacological properties of considerable medical interest. It is, therefore, a matter of great concern that even our star hotels (including those in the public sector) serve not more than 10 vegetables and very rarely fruits such as custard apple or guavas. India has the potential of capturing a vast proportion of the world vegetable and fruit market, if it could only appropriately publicise its rich heritage in this regard, just as the French high-power marketing made bottled water popular around the world, even in countries such as the United States and Britain where there was no bottled water till the 1960s. Therefore, an appropriate task force should be set up for popularizing our traditional fruits and vegetables. This should be done in collaboration with the private sector and the ICAR.

(iv) The Ministry of Tourism should set up a separate cell for ensuring that our traditional practices become major tourist attractions.

(v) We should set up a national mission for creative, cultural and legacy industries which will bring work in these areas under various Ministries (some 10 of them) under one umbrella.

We trust that you would find the above recommendations of value.

With warm personal regards,

Yours sincerely,
Sd/-
(P M Bhargava)

Recommendations on Selected Areas of Traditional Knowledge

CONTENTS

(I)   Principles and Basic Premises

(II) Traditional Medicinal and Healthcare Systems with Special Reference to Plant-based Drugs

(III) Traditional Agricultural Practices

(IV) India's Vegetables and Fruits

(V)   Traditional Practices and Tourism

(VI) Leveraging our Creative, Cultural and Legacy Industries for Employment and Wealth Generation (including Appendix A of this section)

(VII) Meetings held and people consulted

(I) Principles and Basic Premises

The following principles and basic premises should cover all modes of traditional knowledge and should provide the framework for a definitive policy statement by the government in this regard.

(1) In all commercialization of traditional knowledge, there must be equity in respect of distribution of profits. Thus, the producer or the traditional keepers of the knowledge must be considered as equal partners along with others in the commercial exploitation of traditional knowledge. A code of fair trade practices in this area must be evolved by the designated organization.

(2) It must be recognized that traditional knowledge does not need to be collective; it can be with an individual. Similarly, it should not be taken as being static. It must be recognized that innovation takes place constantly even in what we label as traditional knowledge.

(3) Where a marriage of traditional knowledge with what is commonly perceived as modern knowledge is likely to yield better results, it should be ensured that the traditional knowledge component is not lost sight of, either in practice or in publicity.

(4) We must recognize both tangible and intangible variations in any traditional knowledge item, stemming from underlying traditional taxonomy.

(5) Where traditional knowledge comes from identifiable groups or individuals and is not in public domain, prior informed consent of the contributors of the traditional knowledge or innovation must be obtained.

(6) A legal framework should be created for establishing proprietary rights for traditional knowledge holders—be they individuals or a community.

(7) A system should be set up for urgent scientific investigation of traditional practices, including survival strategies, for which there is strong prima facie evidence.

(8) The definition of work for employment purposes must include all activities that relate to the use and application (not just manual but also mental) of traditional knowledge.

(9) A system should be created for support to those who are involved in formal transmission of traditional knowledge – specially women and older people in communities where young people have been migrating to urban areas in large numbers.

(10) A system should be set up that would provide incentives for inter-community transmission/transfer of traditional knowledge to ensure that knowledge is not lost—remembering that knowledge multiplies when shared and decays when kept secret or confidential.

(11) The results of all research and development based on traditional knowledge must be shared with the providers of the initial knowledge package.

(12) Whatever infrastructure is created to document, standardize, validate and use or commercialize traditional knowledge must be cross-sectoral and cross-ministerial; the system set up must operate in a mission mode with cross-sectoral and cross-ministerial powers.

(II) Traditional Medical and Healthcare Systems with Special Reference to Plant-based Drugs

A. Introduction

1. The list of members of the Working Group set up for this purpose, is given in Section G below.

2. A questionnaire was designed and sent to all members of the Discussion Group, most of whom attended a meeting organized by Dr Darshan Shankar, Director, Foundation for Revitalisation of Local Health Traditions (FRLHT), Bangalore, in Bangalore on 6th July 2006. What follows has taken into account the response to the questionnaire and the proceedings of the 6th July meeting in Bangalore.

3. It was agreed that as a first step, we must recognize the following:
   a. A very large percentage of our people use traditional systems of medicine. This is, perhaps, so also in many other developing countries. Even in developed countries, the so-called "alternative" systems of medicine are gaining ground, partly on account of the modern systems of medicine being expensive.
   b. If these (traditional) systems did not have any therapeutic value, mankind would have been wiped out by now, just as if they could cure all diseases that modern medicine can cure, we would have reached today's population several millennia ago.
   c. Therefore, just as traditional systems have helped mankind survive, modern system of medicine has also contributed significantly to the welfare of mankind and certainly to the dramatic increase in the life-span of man by providing means of prevention and cure of diseases.

d. Plant-based formulations have been the main stay of virtually all major (codified or uncodified) traditional systems of medicine.

e. Similarly, yoga has today found wide acceptance within and outside of the country, as not only a highly sophisticated and effective form of physiotherapy, but also as a means of augmenting the feeling of well-being.

f. Besides plant-based formulations and yoga, there are other traditional medical and healthcare practices that are not incompatible with modern science and need to be validated and (at times) standardized.

4. Recommendations that follow in the following few sections are based on what has been said in the three preceding paragraphs about plant-based drug formulations, yoga, and other traditional medical and healthcare practices which do not go against the grain of science.

B. Recommendations

It is recommended that a *national mission on plant-based drug formulations, yoga, and other traditional medical and health practices that are not incompatible with science be set up*, with three sub-missions, one each covering the above-mentioned three areas described in the following three sections.

C. Plant-based drug formulations

Plant-based drug formulations offer the advantage of cost, lack of side effects, and reduced time for validation using today's criteria. In addition, they can be a major source of national pride if commercialized and made available universally.

The challenge lies in integrating plant-based drug formulations and other protocols for prevention and cure of ailments or diseases, or for augmenting the feeling of well-being, that are not incompatible with science, with the modern system of medicine. This would imply, among other things, working towards having plant-based drug formulations become ethical drugs through standardization and validation. The scope for doing so is enormous as there are some 40,000 unique plant-based drug formulations that have come to us through the documented Ayurvedic, Unani, Siddha and Tibetian systems of medicine and the undocumented tribal systems of medicine. At least one detailed project report is available with Dr P M Bhargava, which establishes that it is possible for India to market as ethical drugs a hundred such formulations in ten years, with an annual turnover of about ten thousand crores of rupees. To meet this challenge, it is recommended that a sub-mission be set up under the aegis of the mission mentioned in Section A.

The objectives (terms of reference) of the *Sub-mission on Plant-based Drug Formulations* may be the following:

(a) Computerized documentation of the plant-based drug formulations from all our traditional systems of medicine done in a way that all useful information (e.g. symptom-specific, disease-specific, or plant-specific) can be easily retrieved. We need to bring together the efforts of CSIR, National Innovation Foundation, and FRLHT, along with those of others in this regard, and fill in the lacunae in these documentations. For this purpose, an equivalence of terms used for diagnosis and cure in the language in which the traditional formulation is written, and in English, would need to be worked out.

(b) Setting up of an organization for standardization of the formulations, using *in vitro* systems and Good Laboratory Practice (GLP). Where necessary, the formulations would need to be stabilized by appropriate processing arrived at by research. The formulations would then need to be validated using GCP and also by developing new techniques and methodologies of social validation. They would then need to be manufactured using Good Manufacturing Practice (GMP) and interacting with the Manufacturing Council of India. Finally, they would need to be suitably advertised and marketed nationally and internationally, in which effort the Exim Bank of India could be involved.

(c) Preparation of eco-specific plant pharmacopoeias.

(d) Setting up a system for identification of varieties, standardization of agro-practices including harvesting using GAP (Good Agriculture Practice) and GHP (Good Harvesting Practice), interaction with farmers on a continuing basis (for example, by contract farming), and development of new techniques of propagation of elite plants such as tissue culture. The ICAR could be involved in these efforts.

(e) Provision of aid for establishing community-based herbal gardens. In Vietnam, for example, the primary health centres have such herbal gardens.

(f) Working towards appropriate legislation that would allow allopathic doctors to prescribe traditional drugs or protocols that do not go against the principles of modern science.

(g) Encouraging research, for example, on interaction between various plant-based drug formulations. Two recent studies in this regard are mentioned below.
  • R. Venkatramana, B.Komareski, S. Strom, "In vitro and in vivo assessment of herb drug interactions", *Life Sciences*, 2006, 78 (18), pp. 2105–2115.
  • D. Pal, A.K. Mitra, "MDR and CrP3A4–mediated drug-herbal interactions", *Life Sciences*, 2006, 78 (18), pp.2131–2145.

(h) Introduction of elements of traditional herbal healing and of other traditional products for treatment of diseases, maintenance of health, or augmentation of the feeling of well-being, that do not contradict today's science, in courses in medical colleges of India.

(i) Development of a strategy for appropriate protection of our traditional knowledge in regard to herbal healing, for example by invoking and implementing provisions of Convention on Biodiversity.

(j) Working out a strategy to ensure that there is no misinformation spread about herbal drugs.

(k) Working out strategies for international acceptance.

(l) Provision of validated herbal medicines at low cost to our citizens.

(m) Ensuring that appropriate steps are taken to conserve our medicinally useful plants, for example through tissue culture. The National Medicinal Plant Board could be given this responsibility along with appropriate support.

(n) Setting up a system of certification of herbal medicines and of the various steps involved in manufacturing them from seeds to the final product. ICMR and ICAR could jointly be made nodal agencies for this certification.

(o) Spawning appropriate industries in small, medium and large-scale sectors to meet the above objectives.

(p) Managing a special venture fund that may be set up by the government for the above purpose.

D. Yoga

The sub-mission on yoga should be set up with the following objectives (terms of reference):

(a) To prepare standard and authentic documentation on yoga, including yogic exercises, and stating what the physiological/biological effects of a particular practise may be.

(b) To document on a continuing basis all modern scientific investigations of yoga.

(c) To carry out research, using all available tools and methodology, where needed, to validate/verify/substantiate/augment claims of yoga, and to establish new uses of yogic exercises.

(d) To include yoga in the syllabus of first medical degree in our medical colleges.

E. Other traditional medical and healthcare practices

A sub-mission should be set up on traditional medical and healthcare practices (excluding plant-based drug formulations and yoga) that are not incompatible with modern science, with the following objectives/terms of reference:

(a) To identify such practices from all our traditional systems of medicine and document them at one place, making use of existing documentation in both the government and the NGO sectors.

(b) To validate these practices using appropriate scientifically valid methodologies, where necessary.

(c) To document on a continuing basis existing and new scientific investigations of such practices.

(d) To incorporate such validated practices in the syllabus of first medical degree in our medical colleges.

(e) To carry out research to build on scientifically proven/established and validated practices, with a view to generate new knowledge in the area.

(f) To set up new institutions/organizations as required for the above purposes to popularize such practices.

F. General

The following will be applicable to what has been said in the three preceding sections:

(a) The larger objective of the mission/sub-missions suggested above should be to eventually integrate modern medicine and validated traditional medical and healthcare practices, from the points of view of both medical education and practice, and thus evolve a wholesome system of medicine that combines the advantages of both tradition and modernity.

(b) For the above purpose, where necessary, manufacturing units following GLP and GMP would need to be set up under the auspices of the mission/commission, in the private, public or joint sector, with appropriate incentives in the beginning.

(c) To meet the above objectives, a major national programme of digitising Indian traditional medical manuscripts (be they in India or abroad) would need to be taken up, with the digital library being freely accessible to all those concerned or interested.

(d) Appropriate standards and certifying systems incorporating GCP, GLP, GMP, GAP and GHP would need to be set up that would be applicable to all products/services across the board (Sections C to E) that concern medical and healthcare.

(e) To make the above possible, an initial allocation of Rs.2000 crores should be made for the first five years, after which the system should generate enough resources to take care of provision of medicines or related manufactured products (but not of provision of services). With the above capital, the mission/sub-missions should be able to sustain their activities in the future and even generate resources for the government through royalties so that the above amount is paid back to the government in 10 to 15 years after the first five years, if need be at a low rate of interest.

(f) The mission or sub-mission leader in all the above cases must satisfy the following criteria:

   (i)   high public credibility
  (ii)   extensive knowledge and experience
 (iii)   commitment to the above objectives
 (iv)   appropriate scientific background
  (v)   established managerial capabilities
(vi)   experience of dealing with all the concerned stockholders including the government.

The mission leader should present a ten-year plan with measurable milestones, within six months of the setting up of the mission.

G. Members of the discussion group

1. Mr Ravi Prasad, CEO, Himalaya Drugs (ravi.prasad@ himalayahealthcare.com)
2. Mr Mohammed Majeed, Sami Chemicals (mail@samilabs.com)
3. Mr Ranjit Puranik (rap@sdlindia.com)
4. Mr Amit Agarwal (amit@naturalremedy.com)
5. Dr P.K.Varier (koz_kottakal@sancharnet.in)
6. Mr P.R. Krishnakumar (rajamandiram2003@yahoo.com)
7. Dr Ramesh Varier (avn@eth.net)
8. Dr M S Valiathan (msvaliathan@yahoo.com)
9. Dr Bhushan Patwardhan (bhushan@unipune.ernet.in)
10. Dr G G Gangadharan (vaidya.ganga@frlht.org.in)
11. Dr P M Unnikrishan (unni.pm@frlht.org.in)
12. Dr Padma Venkat (padma.venkat@frlht.org)
13. Dr Lavekar, Director, CCRAS (ccras_dir1@nic.in)
14. Mr A V Balasubramanian (info@ciks.org)
15. Vaidya Vilas Nanal (vilasnanal@yahoo.co in)
16. Dr R H Singh (rau-jod@yahoo.com)
17. Prof. Kumar (kumar@chemeng.iisc.ernet.in)
18. Dr N H Antia (frchbom@bom2.vsnl.net.in, frchpune@giaspn01. vsnl.net.in)
19. Dr Narendra Bhatt (drnsbhatt@vsnl.com)
20. Dr Ashok Vaidya (ab_vaidya@yahoo.co.in)
21. Dr Urmila Thatte (clinpharm@vsnl.net)
22. Mr Vijay Singh, Secretary, AYUSH (secy-ayush@nic.in)
23. Prof. Ranjit Roy Chaudhury (chairinclen@sify.com),
24. Mr Shiv Basant, Jt. Secretary, AYUSH (jsismh@nic.in)
25. Mr B S Sajwan, CEO, NMPB (Bssajwan@yahoo.com)
26. Dr Vasantha Muthuswamy, Sr. Deputy Director General, ICMR (muthuswamyv@icmr.org.in)

27. Mr Samuel Verghese, Joint Secretary, AYUSH (samuelverghese@ yahoo.com)
28. Dr Darshan Shankar, FRLHT
29. Mrs Chandana Chakrabarti, NKC
30. Dr P M Bhargava, NKC

(III) Traditional Agricultural Practices

(1) The Indian Council of Agricultural Research (ICAR) has recently brought out a series of volumes that document 4,502 traditional agricultural practices. Out of these, 86 had been validated and 38 cross-validated till December 2005. The above documentation is in addition to the documentation that the National Innovation Foundation (NIF) has of such practices. Clearly, there is a need to have a consolidated, cooperative system of documentation of these practices, appropriately computerized and indexed, to which anyone can contribute and which anyone can access. Therefore, a national centre for such documentation should be set up under the joint leadership of NIF and ICAR which should be appropriately advertised so that additions could be made to the list from time to time.

(2) The cross-validated practices mentioned above should be commercialized and an *appropriate mission set up for commercialization of traditional agricultural practices, which could begin with the above cross-validated 38 practices.* However, before the above commercialization takes place, appropriate consent of those who contributed to the practice (individuals or communities) should be obtained and a system should be set up (as mentioned under Principles and Basic Premises) for fair sharing of profit as a result of commercialization. This should be the responsibility of the above-mentioned Mission.

(3) A set of strategies for validation should be worked out by the above Mission. For example, one should be able to use and encourage expert farmers to be a part of the validation process; they should be appropriately supported with adequate staff. Farmers who have been honoured and recognized in any legitimate way and whose commitment has not been in doubt should be specially encouraged to be a part of the validation process.

(4) An appropriate venture fund that would support the above-mentioned validation process should be set up by the above Mission.

(5) The above process of validation under the auspices of the Mission mentioned above should not be confined only to what has been documented till now. It must be recognized that innovation by farmers continues to take place all the time. Such innovation could be, for example, in areas as diverse as new agricultural implements, herbal pesticides, veterinary medicines, animal and plant growth regulators, food processing and so on. A nation-wide system should be set up, perhaps in collaboration with NIF, that would ensure that all such innovations come to the notice of the above Mission in real time. The Mission should have a machinery to screen them and those that pass the screening test should then go through the process of evaluation and commercialization as mentioned above.

(6) A system must be set up, perhaps under Plant Varieties Protection and Farmers' Rights Act, to generate the required statistical data for new plant varieties developed by farmers, without any financial burden on the farmers, in respect of a possible *new* use for the varieties. For example, there could be a variety with a different colour of its flower which will repel insects.

(IV) India's Vegetables and Fruits

India has many uncommon vegetables and fruits—and an unparalleled variety of them. Thus, there are some 150 documented vegetables for which nutritional information is available, and perhaps some 50 used by tribals which have not been systematically documented so far. The same is true of fruits. It is, therefore, a matter of great concern that even our star hotels serve no more than some 10 vegetables, and very rarely fruits such as custard apple or guava.

India has the potential of capturing the world vegetable and fruit market, if it could only appropriately publicize its rich heritage in this regard. In this connection, we should recall that there was no (what we call) mineral water available in the United States or in Britain till the 1960s. It was the French high-power marketing that made bottled water (beginning with Evian and Perrier, produced in the French public sector) so popular in these countries, exactly as it has happened in our country, even though in all of them the water that comes through the tap is perfectly drinkable. In our country itself we have seen how South Indian snacks have invaded the North Indian market where they were unknown till the late 1940s. There is, therefore, no reason why India should not exploit its tremendous heritage in regard to foods and vegetables and attempt to popularize them all over the world.

An appropriate task force should be set up for this purpose which should also include Indian industries that may be interested in being a part of the above process. This effort should be undertaken in conjunction with ICAR's effort on development and commercialization of post-harvest technologies including food processing.

An important step that the above-mentioned task force could take is to have a meeting with leaders of the Indian Hotel Industry with the objective of popularizing our vegetables and fruits, making use of rapidly increasing and highly reliable scientific literature on the many useful pharmacological properties of our fruits and vegetables. One of the objectives of the task force would, then, be to scan this literature on a continuing basis and, with the help of the hospitality industry in the country, prepare appropriate material which would be of interest to tourists.

(V) Traditional Practices and Tourism

Our Ministry of Tourism may consider taking the following steps:

(a) Set up a mechanism to empower, through information, local people to serve as guides at all tourist sites in the country. They should also be concurrently trained to be the custodians of our biodiversity heritage. This would be in consonance with the provisions of the proposed Tribal Rights Bill.

(b) Identify tribal art centres where they exist, and open new ones where possible, with competent and trained guides from the local population. Local people have information and anecdotes that the tourists will enjoy.

(c) Set up a system by which tourists are able to witness real and authentic local performing arts at select places, without adulterating them in any way and ensuring that the respect and dignity of the performer is fully maintained. The objective should be to share a tradition and not to make an exhibition of oneself.

(d) Our country has some extremely unusual sites and practices which can become a major tourist attraction. For example, there is a place where birds commit suicide. Similarly, the whole process of picking up the raw betel nuts from a set of betel nut trees is absolutely stunning. Such places could become major tourist attractions. The revenue from the visit of tourists to such places should be shared with the communities involved. The Ministry of Tourism should work out a system for such sharing.

The Ministry of Tourism may set up a special cell for the above purposes.

(VI) Leveraging Our Creative, Cultural and Legacy Industries for Employment and Wealth Creation

A. The Background

Our natural assets are:

- Seven geo-climatic zones
- Vast coastline
- Water bodies
- Rainfall
- Sunlight

- Forests
- Minerals
- Land
- Animal and plant biodiversity
- Natural beauty

Our human assets are:
- Scientific manpower
- Technological manpower
- High-level expertise in virtually all other areas of human endeavour
- Traditional and indigenous knowledge carriers
- Greatest human diversity in the world
- Large number of young people

Our man-made assets are:
- Science
- Technology
- Green Revolution
- White Revolution
- Information Technology revolution
- Space revolution
- Atomic energy revolution
- DNA technology revolution
- Defence technology revolution
- Institution-building revolution
- Drug revolution
- Infrastructure in every sector

Our social assets are:

- Ancient culture
- History
- Variety
- Art
- Handicrafts
- Music
- Dance
- Family set-up
- Closeness of social relations
- Social bonding
- Traditional values
- Tradition of hospitality
- Largest working democracy in the world
- Constitutional strengths

B. Why leverage our creative, cultural and legacy traditions?

We should do so for:

- Employment
- Additional employment
- Revenue for the country
- Enhancing country's prestige
- Research leading to more of the above

The rest of the world is already using its creative and cultural industries to accomplish the above (documentation in this regard can be provided through the Asian Heritage Foundation). As what follows will show our creative, culture and legacy traditions, with an uninterrupted history of

5000 years and unparalleled variety, are the richest in the world, with tremendous potential for meeting the above objective.

C. Final objective

Our final objective should be "aggressive" but ethical marketing of:
- Products (e.g. crafts, textiles, products of household manufacturing, food)
- Services (e.g. design, architecture and building, health and healing)
- Various art forms (e.g. fine arts and studio arts; performing and visual arts; culinary arts)
- Traditional games and sports
- Places of tourist value (including libraries, archives, museums and galleries)
- Knowledge

D. Step 1: Identification and mapping

We should make a comprehensive list of items mentioned in (C) above, and do a complete mapping of each item across the country with all relevant details including location, special features, people employed, present system of revenue generation, and constraints. Some examples follow. For a more detailed (but not truly comprehensive) list, see Appendix A.

Products
- Handicrafts
- Handlooms / Textiles
- Building materials
- Paintings
- Sculpture

- Calligraphy
- Vegetables, fruits (discussed earlier)
- Traditionally processed foods
- Flowers, e.g. orchids
- Validated plant-based drug formulations (discussed earlier)
- Cosmetics
- Jewellery
- Organic food

Services

- Design, decoration, fashion
- Architecture and building arts
- Water harvesting

Various art forms

- Dance (classical & folk)
- Music (classical & folk)
- Theatre and drama
- Circus / magicians / puppetry
- Street entertainment
- Story telling
- Painting
- Sculpture
- Cartoons / caricatures
- Calligraphy
- Culinary arts

Tourism

- Natural beauty
- Historical sites
- Religious sites
- Museums and galleries (public, private)
- Libraries and archives (public, private)
- *Haat*s and bazaars
- Festival
- *Dharmashalas* / families that would accept guests
- Institutions

Knowledge

- Mapping and documentation of all the above on a continuing basis
- Translation of our literature in various languages
- Comprehensive documentation of our ancient texts, their translation and analysis (e.g. for scientific validity)

E. Step 2: Compilation of information (10 years?)

- Encyclopedias
- Books (translation & marketing)
- Tourist material (translation & marketing)

F. Step 3 (Concurrent with Step 2)

- Work out principles and strategies for marketing of each item in Step 1 (e.g. maximum share to producer; fair share to others in the chain who put in their effort)

G. Who? How?

In continuation of the task force set up in the Planning Commission, Government of India, for creative and cultural industries (which was wound up in 2006), a Mission should be set up for the above purposes, with appropriate executive powers, with dedicated and competent people (who will not be transferred frequently), and with a mandate to establish linkages with the concerned industries, NGOs, and Gram Sabhas / Panchayats upwards in the hierarchy of local self government. The power and activities of the Mission would need to transcend inter-ministerial and inter-departmental barriers of allocation of business.

The specific objectives of the above-mentioned Mission on Creative, Cultural and Legacy Industries may be:

(a) Revise the Indian Standards Industrial Code to include the above-mentioned cultural industries and bring it where necessary in accordance with international standards of cultural occupations.

(b) Map and collect all relevant data on a continuing basis in regard to items mentioned in Section D above and in Appendix A. This would need to be done by an appropriate specialized mechanism to be set up.

(c) Remove fragmentation of creative and cultural industries. As of now, they are under nearly 10 different ministries. They should be functionally brought under one appropriate ministry.

(d) Take steps to revise dying skills and upgrade existing skills, using new or existing information, and thus serve as a tool for capacity building.

(e) Set up appropriate training mechanisms—perhaps with the help of the private sector.

(f) Set up a system of providing information, on a continuing basis, to those directly engaged in productive activities in regard to cultural and legacy industries; this information should be both general (that will help the recipient to become a well-informed citizen of the country) and specialized (that would help increase his/her productivity)

(g) Identify the infrastructure support that would be required, and take steps to provide such support. (An example would be setting up of appropriate storage facilities.)

(h) Help set up—both in the private and in the public sector—manufacturing or performing facilities as appropriate.

(i) Set up an effective system of promotion and marketing, making use, for example, of our missions abroad.

(j) Ensure availability and adequate distribution of raw material.

(k) Set up regional and local institutional infrastructure that would help doing what is mentioned above.

(l) Ensure adequate financial support and incentives such as tax concessions and insurance cover where appropriate.

(m) Strengthen the existing copyright and GI protection system that would help those engaged in creative, cultural and legacy industries.

(n) Review existing regulatory mechanisms in the areas covered, with the objective of setting up a separate regulatory/legal authority to be exclusively concerned with cultural, creative and legacy industries.

(o) Examine the habitat and working conditions of those engaged in creative, cultural and legacy industries, with a view to ensuring that these conditions are optimized for maximum productivity and that no aspect of basic human rights (such as child labour laws) is violated.

(p) Be proactive in regard to all the above and ensure that in all the efforts, emphasis on those engaged in creative, cultural and legacy industries and on their products and services is not lost in the maze of bureaucracy and regulatory mechanisms.

(q) Involve relevant NGOs.

(r) The mission should consist of a Chairman, a Vice-Chairman, a Secretary and about seven members. It should include at least one representative of a national NGO and one of an apex organization in one of the areas concerned. All the members should have high public credibility, no vested interests, a wide vision, commitment to the country and to those engaged in creative, cultural and legacy industries, and indisputable personal honesty and integrity. They should have an impeccable record of social service and knowledge that transcends disciplinary barriers. The Chairman should have a high national and international reputation in the field.

Appendix A (of the preceding section)
(Examples of Creative, Cultural and Legacy Industries)

1. Crafts, Textiles and Household Manufacturing

1.A Handicrafts

1.1 Bead / Bangle making

1.2 Blowing Glass

1.3 Carving / Etching / Engraving

1.4 Casting

1.5 Cutwork / Trellis

1.6 Enameling

1.7 Ephemeral expressions (such as *pandals*, bamboo structures, and flower decorations)

1.8   Filigree / Wire work

1.9   Footwear

1.10 Furniture assembly and Carpentry

1.11 Glazing

1.12 Inlay

1.13 Lacquering / Lac turnery

1.14 Lapidary

1.15 Moulding and Shaping

1.16 Paper making

1.17 Plating

1.18 Relief work / Embossing

1.19 Setting / Fixing

1.20 Throwing

1.21 Turning

1.22 Traditional Painting and Frescoes

1.23 Assembly skills (such as Toy making, Jewellery making, and Book binding)

1.24 Pottery

1.25 Paper mache

1.26 Various indigenous uses of plant material such as making of "pattals" (for serving food) and cloth from parts of banana tree

1.27 Toys

1.B   Khadi and Handlooms (and related activities)

1.28 Felt making

1.29 Spinning / Drawing of thread

1.30 Weaving

1.31   Cording / Knotting / Tesselling

1.32   Dyeing / Printing

1.33   Embroidery / Applique / Quilting

1.34   Lace / Crochet / Knitting

1.35   Tailoring

1.36   Costume accessories (Turbans, Bags, Belts)

1.37   Traditional apparel and accessories

1.38   Wool preparation and processing

1.39   Sericulture

1.40   Honey making

1.C   Household manufacturing

1.41   Herbal preparations

1.42   Utility products (chalk, incense)

2. Design, Architecture and Building Arts

2.A   Design

2.1   Graphic design

2.2   Intermedia design

2.3   Industrial / Product / Commercial / Packaging design

2.4   Artistic direction, Scenography, Museography

2.5   Fashion, Costume and accessories design

2.B   Architecture and Building Arts

2.6   Services (Building / Technical and Engineering services), Planning and Survey

2.7   Construction skills and Architectural features (Masonry, Welding and Soldering)

2.8   Conservation and Restoration

2.9   Landscape design

2.10 Interior design

2.11 Community-based systems of Transportation, Sanitation, Irrigation

3. Fine arts / Studio arts

3.1   Painting

3.2   Sculpture and Installations

3.3   Cartoons and Caricature

3.4   Calligraphy

4. Performing and Ritual Arts

4.1   Dance

4.2   Music

4.3   Theatre and Dramatic arts

4.4   Itinerant / Street / Circus arts and entertainment

4.5   Folk performances, Festivals and Rituals

5. Literary Arts

5.1   Oral literature and Story telling

6. Antique Arts and Trade

7. Cultural Education and Training

7.1   Libraries and Archives

7.2   Museums and Galleries

7.3   Cultural centres

8. Advertising and Marketing

    8.1   *Haat*s, Bazaars and Festivals

9. Leisure and Entertainment

    9.1   (Traditional) Games and Sports

10. Food and Culinary Arts

    10.1   Vegetables, Fruits, Food processing

    10.2   Organic Food

11. Health and Healing

    11.1   (Traditional) Systems of healing (e.g. yoga, massages, bone-setting)

    11.2   Beauty and Health care

    11.3   Yoga and Meditation

    11.4   Martial Arts

(VII) Meetings Held and People Consulted

Much of what is contained in the recommendations on previous pages is a consequence of the following:

(i)   A meeting on Traditional Knowledge held at the Centre for Cellular and Molecular Biology, Hyderabad, under the auspices of the National Knowledge Commission on 5th December 2005. This meeting was attended by the following:

    (1)   Dr Anil Kumar Gupta, IIM, Ahmedabad

    (2)   Dr Darshan Shankar, Foundation for Revitalisation of Local Health Traditions (FRLHT), Bangalore

(3) Mr Rajeev Sethi, Vice-Chairman, Planning Commission's Task Force on Creative Industries, Delhi

(4) Dr A K Gogoi, Indian Council of Agricultural Research

(5) Mr M P Ranjan, National Institute of Design, Ahmedabad

(6) Mr Neetu Loond, Ishwar (an Indian textiles exports organization), Paris

(7) Dr P M Bhargava, Vice-Chairman, NKC

(8) Mrs Chandana Chakrabarti, NKC

(ii)   Meeting held in Bangalore on 6th July 2006, mentioned under item II (Traditional, Medical and Healthcare Systems)

(iii) Access to the work done by the Planning Commission's Task Force on Creative and Cultural Industries that was wound up in 2006

(iv) Extensive discussion with Mr Rajeev Sethi and his colleagues at the Asian Heritage Foundation, New Delhi

Notes